I0161381

It Has Been My Honor

JOCELYN C. STEWART, ESQ.

It Has Been My Honor

Copyright © 2023 Jocelyn C. Stewart
Book produced by: Anspach Media
Cover design by: Freddy Solis
Photo credit: Misha Dumov, Tacoma Headshots
Make-up credit: Kaitlin Vigil, Tacoma Make-up Artist
Hair credit: Foxfire Salon and Spa North Proctor

All rights reserved. No part of this book may be reproduced or transmitted in any form or by any means without written permission from the author.

ISBN 13: 978-1-7377355-8-8

Printed in USA

Table of Contents

Thanks...5

Dedication 7

Foreword - **William Cassara** 11

Introduction - **Jocelyn C. Stewart** 15

Chapter 1 - **MEDAL OF HONOR**.................................19

Chapter 2 - **CONSPIRACY THEORIES** 39

Chapter 3 - **BREAKING "RULES"**................................59

Chapter 4 - **RIPPLE EFFECTS** 79

Chapter 5 - **POKE TO THE STOMACH** 93

Chapter 6 - **MEDICAL MOTIONS** 111

Chapter 7 - **TINDER® TERROR** 125

Chapter 8 - **WAKE ME UP WHEN IT'S ALL OVER** 139

Chapter 9 - **FLYING FOR CARPETS** 159

Chapter 10 - **INSTAGRAM® INSANITY** 179

Chapter 11 - **TRUTH SMACKS YOU IN THE FACE**.......205

Chapter 12 - **A FUNERAL WOULD HAVE BEEN BETTER** 221

Chapter 13 - **"HAS BEEN"?**......................................239

About The Author..241

Other Books By The Author 247

About The Firm...249

Jocelyn C. Stewart

Thanks

I want to extend special thanks to David Tarrell for his kind edits, Brendon Tukey for his insight and generous feedback, Noah Moss for listening to my countless stories, Brittany Wood for her hard work that enabled my devotion to this project, and Diana Adjadj for her support and gifting me the title of this book.

Jocelyn C. Stewart

Dedication

I write this book to offer what I hope will be received as a broader part of the narrative that has shaped the image that many have assumed about the military since at least 2007. There are those in society who have accepted certain Congressional agendas that there is an epidemic of sexual assault running rampant in our contemporary military. There is also a growing commonly held belief that military leadership are filled with those who abuse their power, and that those who hold positions of esteem at the highest echelons are not safeguarding justice.

I hope some of what I provide in this collection of factual case stories gives context to that narrative, provides some faces to the otherwise faceless identities of supposed sexual predators, alleged abusive leaders, and wrongdoers within the ranks.[1]

I also aspire that this work helps those who otherwise assume allegation as fact to realize there is so much more to our reality. Accept the truth that false allegations occur more often than they should.

---

[1] Where necessary, I have received client consent to share information related to their cases.

I acknowledge that in joining the discourse that my vantage point includes a bias: when people who self-identify as innocent also have resources, they tend to find people like me. My view of the significant number of false accusations is skewed by the pool of service members who find me for representation. I get it, and I acknowledge it. But even one false allegation is too many.

I have been practicing in military courts-martial since 2005,[2] and I am a huge proponent of change. I am exceptionally passionate about the people who take an oath to serve our great nation.

I have appeared before more than fifty-five Military Judges of various service courts, and I have litigated well over one hundred contested courts-martial since 2005. I

---

[2] In 2005, Ms. Stewart began work as a new trial counsel where she remained in prosecution litigation for twenty-six months. In 2007, she transitioned into military defense work until 2010. In 2010, Ms. Stewart was selected to serve as one of the original fifteen U.S. Army Special Victim Prosecutors. In 2012, she left active duty to pursue private practice in military courts-martial defense. Ms. Stewart founded her own law firm and is the CEO of the Law Office of Jocelyn C Stewart, Corp. As of 2023 the firm consists of three full time attorneys, five part time attorneys, one appellate counsel, a dedicated defense investigator, and support staff. Members of the firm have represented clients of every military service and have defended clients in the U.S., Iraq, Afghanistan, Germany, Italy, Japan, and South Korea. From January 2017 until January 2020, Ms. Stewart also served as adjunct professor of criminal law at The Judge Advocate General's Legal Center and School in Charlottesville, Virginia.

stopped counting when I left active service as a judge advocate in 2012.

My blog[3] is critical of much that goes on in the military justice system, but I believe that if I do not try to improve it, I cannot be an antagonist. This is why I helped to form the non-profit, International Association of Military Defense Lawyers; and also, why I write and publish trial practice books in my Shaping the Battlefield Series.

Being a voice for the oppressed brings change for that individual, but cultivating and contributing to the dialogue and shaping policy are the hallmark of a legacy. Some may remember cases I have won over my career, but I pray more will see the benefit of a life spent trying to change the system before the system changed me. It truly has been my honor.

---

[3] https://www.ucmj-defender.com/blog

Jocelyn C. Stewart

Foreword

William Cassara

For over 30 years, I have represented service members in a variety of legal matters, from courts-martial to administrative hearings, to appeals of court-martial convictions. I first met (then) Captain Jocelyn Stewart when she was a young defense counsel. I was presenting at a conference in San Diego to uniformed defense counsel about how to preserve the military appellate record. At the time, I was actively representing military members in courts-martial, a job I now gladly leave to younger lawyers. While the details of our introduction escape me, I recall her desire to learn and to be the best for her clients. I remember several conversations with her in which she simply wanted to pick my brain. Her desire to learn was obvious. Her reputation as a young prosecutor was that she was aggressive but fair. The job of a prosecutor is to do justice, not just to get convictions. Jocelyn seemed to know that, even back then.

Jocelyn and I have remained friends since that day, and when she decided to leave active duty and go into private practice, she reached out to me. Those of us civilian attorneys who practice military law are a small, cohesive group for the most part. I have often called us "competimates." We are competing for the same clients, but we are also fighting the same fight, and most of us are willing to help each other out and bounce ideas off each other. Once again, Jocelyn wanted to learn, and to be a better lawyer.

As defense lawyers the most common question we get is "how do you defend someone who you know is guilty?" I often retort with "why don't you ask the prosecutors how they prosecute someone they know is innocent?" I am often met with blank stares. I don't mean it as harsh as it sounds. But the world and especially the military needs a strong, vibrant, independent defense bar. Our service members need defense lawyers who are not worried about their next promotion, or about whether they are rocking the boat. There is an inherent conflict in the military justice system where, like every other military job, lawyers rotate duty positions every two years. Going from defense counsel to prosecutor is common. There is no career path for defense counsel. A recent high-profile case out of the Marine Corps exemplified that problem, when a senior JAG (Judge Advocate General) warned defense counsel about being too zealous and said, "we know where you work." The implication was that spending too much time as a defense counsel was harmful to your career.

Unfortunately, this was not an isolated case. While most uniformed defense counsel zealously advocate for their clients the perception although not the reality in my experience, is that they are part of the system that is working against the accused. The reality is that they are often overworked, inexperienced and only on a particular assignment for two years.

The need for zealous civilian defense counsel has never been stronger than it is today. Every time Congress passes a new law aimed at military justice, it takes away another right of the accused and presumed innocent service member. Without people like Jocelyn, they may not get that. Jocelyn is a tenacious warrior for her clients. She is the epitome of a "zealous advocate." When we speak about one of her cases, her empathy for her clients is always obvious. Don't mess with her.

As noted earlier, I now concentrate my practice on courts-martial appeals. I don't see many of Jocelyn's cases because, well, she doesn't lose often. But even in the times when I have seen one of her cases on appeal, I can be certain that it was well tried, and that she did everything in her power to advocate for her client. All too often I see defense counsel withdraw objections because they are badgered by a military judge. Not so with Jocelyn. She has never been afraid to go toe to toe with military judges and assert her position. While a judge may rule against her, she will "preserve the record" as we appellate lawyers say. This is invaluable on appeal.

In this book you will read several of Jocelyn's "war stories." It is hard for us lawyers to retell these stories without coming across as bragging. She isn't. She is telling the truth, in the hope that younger lawyers can learn from her and to be part of a broader narrative to ensure the public knows that we represent the innocent too. Both of us are frequently asked to give presentations to young defense counsel on trial and appellate strategies. Her knowledge base is extensive, and she is more than willing to share her talents with other "competimates."

I enjoyed this book. Even at my age, I learned things, both about Jocelyn and the practice of law. I hope you enjoy this book. I have no doubt that you will learn something new.

- William Cassara

Introduction

Jocelyn C. Stewart

I never believed in my wildest dreams that I would grow a law firm of private attorneys who fight for justice in an often unjust military system. Mostly because I didn't have dreams, wild or otherwise.

I have grown into dreaming, into imagining, into realizing that I am a force. I didn't hear it at home. In my formative years, the echoes of my mother's words after I lost yet another school government election: you will never win. Why do you keep putting yourself out there? You will never win. Boy was she wrong.

I have sincere gratitude for the words of those whose voices grew louder than those maternal ricochets. I revel in a conversation with a dear friend as a I recalled the idea someone posited that I would mostly be a mom with a part-time / hobby type profession of private court-martial practice. "Does he actually know you?" she chided. That's right. I really only do things one way: all the way. And I really have. Thank heaven for therapy and escaping narcissism and cruelty. Even if it took me almost 40 years.

I give the deepest thanks for the roads that led me to every client, and I know in my quietest moments that each one was meant to be. This does not serve to undo the profound gratitude for the tango of trust when clients choose me, and we work together to find justice.

I often tell "war stories" about the cases I have tried. I think most trial attorneys do. Most recently, I have undertaken to tell them on a new platform to share some of my stories on social media.[4] I show some of the necklaces I buy to commemorate my wins. Elva Fields® is my trusted source for these one-of-a-kind beauties. These treasures help me remember each client as I go into battle, enveloped in their stories of triumph, comforted that I am never alone in the battle to seek truth.

In whichever forum, I am strengthened by having had the opportunity to tell their story, to champion their cause, and to stand up for them in court, in military hearings, and sometimes in merely words on a page.

No matter how long I have been in this job, I continue to marvel at the amazing people who entrust me with their reputation, livelihood, and liberty. I feel enormously fortunate to have crossed paths with each one; every

---

[4] TikTok: @MessyMilitaryLawyer; Instagram: messymilitarylawyer

person has taught me invaluable lessons. While each war leaves me weary, I am strengthened by their unwavering trust, and I am renewed by their resilience.

There is no greater calling, and representing each of the otherwise silenced as their gladiator in the arena has been my highest privilege.

It has been my honor.

- Jocelyn C. Stewart –

* In 2012, Ms. Stewart left active service to pursue a private practice dedicated to defending servicemembers worldwide, with particular emphasis in sexual assault investigations and sexual assault court-martial defense. As a civilian court-martial and military administrative matter specialist, she has represented clients all over the world, from the west coast to the east coast, the gulf coast, and the Midwest, Europe, Asia, and the Middle East. Her clients serve the Army, the Air Force, the Navy, the Marine Corps, and even the Coast Guard. She patiently awaits her first client from the Space Force. Her firm's[5] mantra is that they want to be where they can do the "most good."[6]

---

[5] Law Office of Jocelyn C Stewart, Corp. www.ucmj-defender.com

[6] https://www.ucmj-defender.com/we-want-to-be-where-we-can-do-the-most-good-for-military-justice/

Jocelyn C. Stewart

Chapter 1

MEDAL OF HONOR

I nearly missed out on representing one of the most honorable men I have ever known because I was setting a boundary. Sort of.

I had already missed a Sunday walk to the neighborhood school park with my then spouse and our three young children. P.S. I had a fourth child with him before awakening fully to myself.

Sitting in the shame and reverberating guilt of choosing work over family, I had a consultation with a potential client. Then I planned to catch up to them at the park. See? I could have it all... Catch may be generous; I was actually pregnant at that time with our fourth child.

I was finishing up an email to send with a proposed fee agreement when my phone started to ring. And by ring, I mean blow up. I recognized the caller as a current client. I did not answer. Boundaries, I reminded myself. There are no such thing as legal emergencies, I reiterated internally. I had time with my family I needed to prioritize. I was getting many reminders of that. Daily.

Then the phone rang again. I sent it to voicemail. The phone rang again. Being really unlike this client, I picked up. But I began the call by cutting him off, telling him that whatever it was really needed to wait. Boundaries, my new-ish mantra.

He quickly explained that the police were at his friend's door, and his friend needed to know what to do. I was confused. How do you know the police are at his door? He is at the friend's house. Are they there for you? No, something about the friend. Is he in the military? Yes, he is in the same Special Forces unit as my client.

Okay, I relent. I'll talk to him. I am grateful that I did.

From what I could understand in the brief call the police were at the door. Seriously. I have been quoted often as saying "there are no legal emergencies…unless [maybe] the cops are at your door." And even then, if they have a warrant, there's not a whole lot that I can do.

But I always tell them to say "Lawyer" and nothing else. And never consent to anything.

I talk through the issue as quickly but calmly as we can given that the police are at the door. They have a warrant to look for "stolen military property." They are looking for a scope that fits on a firearm.

I would later learn that while on deployment, a civilian contractor (let's call him "Bob") gave my client a scope. That is the least strange fact you'll come to learn in this chapter.

After the frenzied phone call, I set a time to meet up with this new would-be client at a coffee shop near where I was operating out of a home office. Fancy. You are impressed. Still growing into my own, remember?

My first glimpse of (then) Staff Sergeant Earl Plumlee in the coffee shop: a bit of a sideways smile and if you looked closer, pain. Not pain that complained, pain that was an accepted reality with a dash of discomfort at anyone looking too closely. His attire was fairly non-descript. He wore unassuming "civilians."

Because of our location in the back of the coffee shop, albeit on soft leather chairs, I tried to address him in hushed whispers. But he couldn't hear me. As we spoke in louder tones, he apologized multiple times for his not being able to hear and understand me, for requesting that I repeat myself. I also can still see him having to shift from being seated to standing and then shift in his positioning while standing during our meeting. While I would later learn the origin of his pain, I must admit I didn't fully appreciate it, nor did I understand how it would carry significant pressure to ensure this client would be unscathed by the system.

The explanation about why the military was concerned about a scope that Earl had put up for sale on eBay® seemed a little thin. A concerned military member had apparently seen the item for sale and called in a tip line that the scope "could only be military property."

The police were now looking for the scope. When they executed the search warrant at Earl's house, they didn't find it.

This is one of those moments in the life of a criminal defense attorney when you pause before allowing yourself to receive additional information or asking for information. I have always subscribed to the school of thought that when I defend someone, I want to know all the things: good, bad, or indifferent. Did I really want to know the location of this scope? Sigh. I did. Am I sure? He cautions. Oh boy.

Before learning more about its current whereabouts, I explain to Earl this scope needs to be safeguarded, that under no circumstance can I counsel him to get rid of it or to tell anyone else to get rid of it. Sometimes that can sound an awful lot like an attorney telling a client to get rid of a thing without telling the client to get rid of a thing. This was not that case.

I was percolating between two potential defenses: either 1) Earl had no idea the scope was military property because he received it under circumstances that did not indicate that it was; or 2) that it was not, in fact, military property. Under either scenario, I needed to evaluate the scope. If the property was not military property, we needed the property to show it was good old fashioned civilian property. If not military property, it belonged to Earl, and ergo was not stolen.

Earl was a member of a Special Forces team. He still is a part of the community, but I am unclear of his role today. When I say team, or rather when they say team, that means something significant. We aren't talking about a group of guys who assemble for the joint endeavor of getting a frisbee down a field or who play bad softball before beers once a week. A Special Forces team is composed of highly skilled, highly trained specialists who each play a vital role individually and collectively in furthering interests abroad. Sometimes those are clandestine, and sometimes they are well coordinated for show.

In my career, when I am chosen to stand up for any one of these heroes, I steel myself against the easy temptation to be a fan girl. They exist. There are terms used to call these gals, but I'll leave that where it is now. The members of this elite group, like me, are professionals in our given area of expertise. We would all do well to remember this truth.

When I sit around and swap stories – in the south we call this "visiting" – with members of the Special Forces community, I always, and I mean always, mock the majority of military lawyers we call judge advocates who become assigned to Special Forces organizations. It is as though these uniformed attorneys – usually the O-3s – think by being around these elite forces, the "jags" suddenly believe themselves to be "Special" too. They are not. Typically, they are physically fit individuals, but there is a particular danger in coming to believe that by proximity, they are outside the standards of their own organization. They are usually capable at the lawyering part; usually.

With the more senior judge advocates, you will also see instances when they are not the best lawyers with the most legal acumen either. But gosh, they sure can run fast. I would love to name drop some of those fast runner lawyers, but I won't. I would also love to name drop the names of at least two judge advocates who work with clandestine forces, two who are among the best men and lawyers with whom I have ever been proud to serve. Impeccable legal minds. But I won't out them either. Their work is too important.

Rant aside.

So, I am there in this coffee shop just starting to unravel the puzzle about this scope. Apparently, concerned with the impacts of revealing the scope's location, Earl came to this meeting without specifically knowing where the scope was either. That's actually not a terrible move.

After I let that digest, Earl explains that it is being safeguarded. He asks me do I want to know who has it. I say no. As long as he does, and that he knows it is being safeguarded, that is enough for now. He also asked me if I wanted to personally safeguard it. Fuck no. That's a pretty quick method to lose one's law license.

Plus, if it were in my possession, there are certain potential obligations that might make defending his case more difficult than I would like.

My growing concern is allegations of obstructing justice. For him, and maybe some for me. My secondary concern is the ethical quandary if I know the location where evidence of an alleged crime is being housed. Law school hypotheticals can go south quickly in "the field."

After ruminating on the issue and allowing my mind to work out each scenario we could choose, I lay out the plan. It would be a research race. Without taking possession of the scope or learning of its whereabouts, I needed as much information as possible about the scope. My office began calling the manufacturer, trying to ascertain if any of this particular scope had ever been sold to Uncle Sugar. By the way, they don't like handing out that kind of information. My southern charm got my foot in the door, but I would need the serial number. Cool, I can do that. Or so I thought.

Let's avoid the details, but what is most important is that at some point, there had been a serial number on the scope. And then there wasn't. Double sigh. But Earl had nothing to do with the loss of the serial number. Friends trying to be friends often make my job harder.

Remember that part about elite teams? It matters, and there's a reputation that is mostly deserved that team members protect team members. But this was not helpful.

It made my job infinitely harder. There were multiple swear words and maybe even some heart palpitations to commemorate this fact.

Around this time, I learned why in particular people were willing to help Earl. Earl never told me. He wouldn't. Really, he couldn't.

Maybe the title of this chapter tipped you off, but Earl Plumlee was a pending nominee for the Medal of Honor. Do I really need to explain how big of a deal that is? It's huge.

In sitting with the idea of whether this knowledge would crush me in pressure, I need to tell a quick story. I know, you're shocked.

On 5 November 2009, I was stationed as a uniformed defense counsel at Fort Hood, Texas. The day Major Nidal Hasan shot and killed 13 people in the name of a religious war he was fighting in his own mind. My boss, the senior defense counsel, was in D.C. for the Trial Defense Service leadership conference. That means all the leadership was there. Although I was not technically the most senior person among our team, I had been left in charge of the office while the boss was out of town.

The first news reports coming in proclaimed three active shooters acting in concert. I am to get a sit-rep – we call that an update – for where all of us are on the installation: the defense paralegals, the lawyers. According to TDS headquarters, the first shooter to request a lawyer gets me. I am tasked with detailing or assigning the other two. Can I go outside of our installation but stay within our region? No, they say. Um, well, that's going to be a problem…

While this was all happening and before all the cell towers would be jammed, I reached out to a law school mentor. His name is Jim Boren, and he was once the best criminal defense lawyer in Louisiana. I only say was because he no longer practices the purest form of criminal defense, although he does still handle cases in the white collar arena from time to time from what I hear.

My fear was being tasked to defend a capital murder case and feeling unprepared for the weight of that immense burden. As a criminal defense attorney, I speak often of the weight of another person's life in my hands. When it is the death penalty, that is not hyperbole.

Jim takes my call, reminds me to breathe, and tells me this suspect rights is the same as any other in a homicide case, and probably not unlike all others for criminal defense. Period. And just like that, he reminds me that whether the accusation is mass murder or larceny of an eraser, the pressure is the same. Mighty for all. And if it isn't, then I should not be defending anyone.

Side story concluded…

I needed to remind myself that knowing that Earl was a pending candidate for the Medal of Honor was another fact for me to know. Awareness of his candidacy was a consideration to help me make the best tactical decisions for the end goal of keeping Earl Plumlee from being titled and indexed as a subject. People would update me what they knew about where Earl's nomination was in the ever-slithering process for approval. Though tangentially helpful, I could not allow that status to overtake other considerations. If I gave off a sense of entitlement on his behalf or worse arrogance to his reality, I could alienate the decision makers and foreclose this part of his future.

We had few leads to try to find "Bob" – you remember him, the contractor who gifted the scope. Suddenly, that part of the story made much more sense. You see, when people perform such valiant displays of heroism as did Earl Plumlee, people gravitate to that light. People want to show gratitude, and the "dark and twisty" part of me also suspects it is a way for people to feel that they were somehow a part of it.

Earl and I prepared a statement to give to military law enforcement. We authored a factual account of the origin of his possession of the scope and all the information we could provide about it, including our best description of the contractor we call "Bob." I also scheduled a time for us to take the statement to Army CID.

As I have replayed that visit to CID over in my mind since it happened those many years ago, I imagine the prelude. One or more agents who knew my, ahem, reputation knew this would not be an actual interrogation. I had said as much in my electronic communication setting up the appointment. In my mind's eye, I envision those agents separately and unrelatedly also being annoyed with one of their co-workers. Let's assign that guy, they must have decided. Enter Special Agent Sun Moon. Yes, that's his name. Sue his parents, not me.

Agent Sun Moon was incredibly special in his approach. I provided him with the CID Form 44 already completed. This is the biographical sheet the agents "need" filled out and used to build rapport with suspects before working them over to waive their rights and to try to gain admissions. I always get these forms filled out ahead of time, since my presence there is a pretty clear indication there will not be any building of rapport. That done, I hand over the written statement that Earl and I had prepared. All that is left is for Sun Moon to swear Earl to his statement. Before I can explain, as I always do, if there are any follow up questions after the team reviews the statement, those can be directed to me, Sun Moon decides to shoot his shot at some kind of confession. Seriously.

The time it ordinarily takes in the room to advise my client in writing, have him sign on the correct places to waive in part those rights to provide a statement, to hand over said statement and to swear him to it, takes roughly about 5 minutes total in the room. We are on camera, and everything is being audio and videotaped.

Before we can close out, Sun Moon begins what can only be described as a legendary interrogation in his own mind. I have thrown him "off his game" by not letting him build rapport. There's no warmup. He seems flustered. Then he just starts screaming at Earl that he knows he is guilty of stealing the scope and trying to sell it on eBay®.

Wait, what?

I intervene. I am louder.

Earl is stifling laughter.

I have no doubt this recording is on the best hits list of any agent who's ever learned of its existence. Or it definitely should be.

Earl and I exit moments later. Thanks, gents. That was interesting.

I explain to the agents supervising Sun Moon that a way for us all to get to the other side of this unfortunate investigation is that Earl needs to be listed as "witness" in the report, rather than as a "subject." Have you ever had a conversation where someone did not have a clue what you were talking about because you could see it in the quick movement in their eye with an even quicker rebound to try to reassure you in their demeanor that of course they were all over it? Yeah, that.

When I mentioned listing someone as a witness instead of as a subject, that was all over their faces. They did not know it was an option not to list a suspect as a subject. That should stun, trouble, and even offend all readers.

Titling and indexing a person as a subject are among the cruelest aspects of revenge in a military justice system that founds nearly every case and haunts its members for 40 years in a national database that makes other agencies assume their guilt. It ruins chances to work later in law enforcement, and often prevents the purchase of firearms. For Earl, it most certainly would cost him the Medal of Honor.

Not on my watch. Or so I would think.

A few weeks later – we call that record speed for any investigation – CID closes the case. Earl is listed as a witness and not a subject. Case unfounded.

I was incredibly proud of this role that I had played in saving Earl's well-earned, well-deserved nomination. I could tell you the things he did to merit his nomination, but I would embarrass myself because my explanation would not fairly capture its breadth. Look him up if you haven't already. You'll get chills.

The Sergeant Major from Earl's Special Forces Group asked me for 800 of my business cards. He even invited me to come and address the entire Group to tell them why they should never deal with military law enforcement on their own. I respectfully declined his requests, but both invitations remain in my kitbag of where I reach when I have been crapped on by yet another 25-year old military prosecutor or worse an ungrateful client.

I thought everything was going to be okay. At least, I had done my part, and Earl's nomination should sail through the process unscathed. And it did, until it didn't.

At the last moment, Earl Plumlee's richly and justly deserved nomination for the Medal of Honor was downgraded two levels to a Silver Star.

I would like to say that I couldn't believe it, but in candor, I have seen more injustice than justice. And nothing surprises me anymore. But it still breaks my heart.

Earl reached out to invite me to be there with him when he was to receive his Silver Star. It is one of the greatest disappointments of my overly busy life that I could not make that happen. He was a man who everyone knew deserved the highest honor, and I did not want him to field this experience without hopefully the one person who knew and understood this injustice and was even more irate than the entirety of the community who knew the politics that had robbed him. I did not want him to feel alone. That day or any other.

And if you know Earl Plumlee, or any other American hero, he did not save the lives he saved with valor in Afghanistan to have any piece of metal pinned to his chest. But we knew that what had happened in the downgrading was not right. The fury, I cannot properly convey it.

After my formal role on his case had ended, Earl got in touch to tell me that people were approaching him to inquire about filing a complaint or demanding an investigation into the why of the downgrading. He asked me what I thought, and he asked if I could help him field both.

I declined. But not because I didn't feel righteous in either and both. I knew I was in over my head, and that I am not someone who should take on what amounts to a public relations circus. I encouraged Earl to sit with all of it, to quietly allow his mind and heart to lead him where he needed to go. He probably made a clever retort. I was sad to not take up this part of the fight with him and for him. I am not someone to back down from a fight, but I am intensely aware of which ones I am equipped to field. And it just was not mine to contest.

I would follow what happened next in the press. The Washington Post reported it closely, including that Earl's downgraded award supposedly related to his rank as an NCO, instead of as a lower enlisted. They also touched on Earl's investigation for the eBay® scope.

People who believed in Earl, and all of us who disbelieved the Congressionally backed investigation's conclusion that the downgrade was not related to the CID process, knew the truth. That no one wanted the awardee to have been sullied by even an accusation. The hallmark of injustice. A slap in the face to all of us who want desperately to believe that the system, although susceptible to twists and turns, largely gets it right. The reality is the system fails too many.

Somehow in the aftermath of the BS findings of that internal investigation, conversations were had, leverage points were flexed, and the powers that be decided Earl Plumlee's Medal of Honor nomination warranted another look. A new fiscal year and all.

When Earl Plumlee rightfully received the Medal of Honor on December 16, 2021, there was nowhere else I would have wanted to be. Despite Earl's wishes, his desire to have me there did not match his ability. That ceremony, in the height of COVID-19, had limited capacity. I would not make the final tally.

We exchange an occasional text or email. My favorite are the random photographs of Earl with a cigar dangling out of his mouth, holding an indiscernible to me weapon in hand. Just Earl being Earl. He also sends me client referrals. Quite a few. When a Special Forces team member gets through to me for a consultation, I always ask how this person found me. When he replies, Master Sergeant Earl Plumlee, I always accept the case. It is the smallest debt I can repay to the man who allowed me to champion his innocence and to ensure that his story was not tarnished by the misplaced suspicion of a random Soldier online.

To have been part of Master Sergeant Earl Plumlee's journey, however small, was my honor.

Chapter 2

CONSPIRACY THEORIES

We were running late. With four small kids in tow, each dressed in coordinating winter holiday attire, all the cuteness could excuse almost anything.

Trying to step across the snow-packed icy parking lot to the Office of the Staff Judge Advocate holiday party on Joint Base Elemendorf-Richardson, my phone rang. Are you seeing a pattern yet?

Because of course my phone rang. I knew the emotional debt I'd be forced to pay later for taking the call. Did I mention escaping narcissism? I took the call anyway, and it was not one I would ever forget.

A hushed female voice confirmed that I was who I was. And then directed me to Google® "Heather Cole," and then to call her back at this number. Then, she hung up the call.

I remember looking around like I was in an episode of Punk'd®. Seriously. Very cloak and dagger.

My curiosity, ever the puzzle solver, kicked in, and I went to sit in my car to try to keep warm from the chilling wind. This was an Alaskan winter after all.

The Google® results really confused me. Conspiracy theories abounded. The top stories related that President Obama had ordered Navy Captain Heather Cole to launch a nuclear missile at Russia, that she refused the order, and then had been removed from her command for refusing to "nuke" Russia. Attention caught.

I sifted through the Google® returns a bit more. I even found a Facebook® fan page dedicated to freeing Heather Cole from the government oppressors.

Was this CAPT Cole who had called me? Or some fan girl of hers?

The only fairly reliable article I could find was a quick blurb on a military website about CAPT Cole being suspended from her command of an organization at Tinker Air Force Base, Oklahoma. A little more digging uncovered that this particular unit was charged with the Navy's air nuclear capability.

I did what any compulsive puzzle seeker / problem solver-attorney would. I called her back.

There were significant limitations to what we could discuss on an unsecured line. Yes, it would be a case that would have those kinds of implications. Eventually, CAPT Cole and her then partner flew to my office in Tacoma, and they spent three consecutive days doing an extensive "brain dump" so that I could try to comprehend the complexities, undercurrent, and nuances of the investigation that Heather was facing. More importantly, they were helping me to grasp the context and the motivation for what I would come to accept and wholeheartedly understand was the effort by multiple personnel strategically to undermine CAPT Cole's credibility. That's fancy words for take her out before anyone would believe the truth she was trying to speak.

During this "brain dump", I sat at my desk typing nearly verbatim notes for more than eight hours each day for almost three consecutive days. Occasionally, I would stop to ask a question, continue in my note taking, and proceed to receive data. Lots of it.

Anyone who has ever watched me work a case can attest that I am a quick typist. Apparently, I am also described as being an angry typist. I can at least admit that I am deliberate with my keystrokes. One prosecutor tried to object to my typing from the gallery in a co-accused case in Germany. Judge E.J. O'Brien asked me to "keep it down a little."

The conspiracy theories I read online about Heather's command of the Navy's air nuclear capabilities were not accurate. And yet, they were not entirely off.

CAPT Cole had become a target for being discredited when she demonstrated integrity and personal courage, two traits we are supposed to require in leadership. Instead, they – and I do mean "they" – tried to silence her.

Part of Heather's job is to assess nuclear capability as it relates to global threats. For the first, and what I know of, only time in our nation's history, CAPT Heather Cole authored her report that is supposed to be forwarded to the President of the United States and indicated that at the time of her command U.S. nuclear capability was "red." That means what you think it means.

She was immediately ordered to change her report. She conferred with her boss and mentor who reminded her that only she had the authority to make the assessment and that she was duty-bound, as she knew, to report the information accurately. National security relied on it. She refused to change her report. And the powers of the government unleashed hell fire down on her. It came in the form of trumped up ethics violations after being made to wait for charging, more than four years under investigation.

Heather Cole was my client for five and a half years. I have never known someone to be so brilliant and humble simultaneously.

The infinite rage that welled up inside me at the wrongs she was being made to endure was tempered by her faith. Heather's deep faith in God guided every decision she's made and continued to be a source of calm for me.

I knew we needed to be careful, intentional, and patient as we navigated the brewing storm.

What would start as a bizarre conspiracy theory would reveal itself as an actual conspiracy that reached the highest levels of government. I know with certainty that Heather's report was altered before it reached President Barrack Obama's desk. The government would dismiss the case after a series of events, including when we won a motion to discover the report that made its way to the commander in chief. We had the one she sent.

The biggest challenge that I faced in serving – and I do mean serving – as Heather's advocate was knowing when and how to leverage the reality of what was the backdrop and the why behind the onslaught.

The military authorities, when they would speak to me, alleged that they were waiting for the US Attorney's Office to complete their investigation. That took years. When we finally learned that the US Attorney's office would not touch this case with a ten foot pole, the military prosecutors refused to turn over even the memo they had received articulating their ceding of jurisdiction. The government lawyers fought us on everything we had ever requested.

When the military finally charged Heather, the charge sheet was a colossal mess. The allegations ranged from conspiring to wrongfully receive compensation for representational services to improperly using government email for her personal business. There were also charges of her being derelict in the performance of her duties by failing to obtain permission to operate her personal business and conduct unbecoming for all of the above, none of which she did. The initial discovery they provided was upwards of 10,000 pages. Significant portions of the paper on the case were print offs of several government contracts. At the time, it was difficult to decipher which contracts they placed into the case file. Looking back at the cluster later, their only apparent choices were made to include all contracts Heather's company had bid on.

Understand that Heather had owned a business for decades. There is nothing illegal, immoral, or unethical about it. She had complied with the notice, permission, and filing requirements about her business at every command she had ever served. We reached out and obtained proof of her compliance as part of our independent defense investigation. The Navy Public Affairs office had been guided by the Navy lawyers and splashed her name across headlines, all announcing that she had been self-dealing Navy and Marine Corps contracts to her company Worksaver©. The charge sheet also claimed that Heather had misused government resources to include government email and flying on Navy jets when they claimed she should have flown commercially.

After charging her with an eye toward a general court-martial, a felony level criminal trial, the government is required to conduct a preliminary hearing. These are presided over by one senior officer who is almost always senior to the person charged. They must review the evidence submitted by the government and by the defense, if any, listen to any witnesses called for the limited purpose of examining the incredibly low probable cause standard, and produce a report of the findings and recommendations as to disposition.

The first preliminary hearing held under Article 32(b) of the Uniform Code of Military Justice was scheduled two weeks after handing over the results of a four-year long investigation. The initial prosecutor with whom I was interacting understood the volume of materials, my schedule, and other commitments, and personally supported my delay request for an additional six or eight weeks.

His boss did not. Navy CAPT Donald C. King insisted this preliminary hearing take place on a date less than two weeks from the date of charging. Aside from not having sufficient time to prepare to meet this evidence, because of other hearing and trial conflicts I could not possibly attend.

I think that CAPT King thought I would somehow cave and magically show up. He was wrong. He insisted that the Navy could proceed with the Article 32(b) without me, with CAPT Cole being represented solely by her detailed defense counsel. I don't think the assigned military counsel had even tried to read any of the discovery.

I tried diplomacy. Which is rare for me. I reached out to CAPT King to try to explain the long term attorney-client relationship I had with Heather, to reason with him about giving me more time. He refused a phone call, instead sending terse emails demanding that I adhere to the timeline.

My next inclination was to advise Heather to fire her military counsel. This threat had worked in the past when the government was being unreasonable about scheduling. It would seem I needed to launch this "missile." Ah, irony.

I participated in a phone call with the parties and the hearing officer prior to the convening of the Article 32(b) preliminary hearing. I sent a few warning shots to the hearing officer that I felt she was potentially acting against her bar license if she held the hearing without me. She had not even known there was a scheduling issue at all. She was sympathetic and asked if we minded her calling CAPT King to try to resolve the issue and to push the hearing to the right. She said if she was successful, she would alert the parties of this resolution. We never heard from her about the issue again. It seems her efforts at diplomacy and reason had been as well received as ours.

Instead of advising Heather to fire the military defense counsel, I went with a hybrid approach. I had Heather direct the military defense counsel that he did not have any authority to represent her in the hearing. Pursuant to the

Rules for Courts-Martial, as civilian counsel I am the lead counsel, and any detailed counsel is my associate counsel. I gave the assigned uniformed counsel explicit instructions that he was only to read a prepared statement, that he was not at the hearing in any representative capacity, and to file my explicit and robust objections about holding the hearing in my absence.

In proceeding with the preliminary hearing against CAPT Cole's Sixth Amendment right to the counsel of her own choosing, the message was clear: CAPT King had directives from on high to move this case.

So, the Article 32(b) was held without me. At least the first one. Hem hem... The military counsel dutifully refused to say anything past the four corners of the documented statement I had prepared for him. The hearing officer held the hearing, claimed in her report that CAPT Cole had been represented by military counsel, which plainly was at worst a fabrication and at best rather disingenuous. The government counsel presented a stack of papers and put on no witnesses. The defense presented no defense. How could we? I wasn't there, remember?

I recall Heather expressing some initial level of hesitation and concern about my strategy, but she said she had hired me for a reason. She would trust that I was making the right moves.

After the sham prelim, the government referred Heather's case to a general court-martial.

That meant the next stop was the first round of motions to file in the case. There were so many. I fired them off like a well-orchestrated offensive. The most crucial to win would be motions to compel discovery of classified documents, chief among them the report that President Obama had received about Naval air nuclear capability and the motion for a new, or an actual, Article 32(b) preliminary hearing.

I had some concerns about the presiding military judge. I had not appeared before him on any prior cases, and he had been linked to a scandal at the Naval Academy when he had testified in a fairly notorious board of inquiry. Evidence indicated that he had potentially perjured himself, although findings of a formal investigation concluded he had not intentionally lied.

The first session with the court allayed any concerns that I had. He was a pillar of righteous indignation as far as the defense was concerned. I think his prior need to sidestep the landmines he was facing when the investigation into his truth and veracity may very well have prepared him for his role in the CAPT Cole case.

The other significant event that had happened was that the lead counsel who was appointed as the lead prosecutor for CAPT Cole's case had also been the lead counsel for *U.S. versus Eddie Gallagher.* Plenty has been written on that case, but I will share that the entire prosecution team went under investigation for questionable moves to include facilitating a federal tap on the Gallagher defense team's emails. While that played out, this lead prosecutor had been removed from CAPT Cole's case also. I presumed the Navy would find another experienced prosecuting attorney for Heather's trial. They did not. At least not for motions. And most certainly not for the new Article 32(b) preliminary hearing to be.

During the litigation on the motion to compel discovery, the inexperienced trial counsel articulated to the judge that he had denied most if not all of the discovery we were arguing about because he did not know what the items were. Seriously.

The judge suggested that before denying production of a document, a better practice might be to research what the item was, or better, to pick up the phone to call the defense to ask us to explain the significance. A nice idea, though I am not certain I would have taken the time to connect the dots for them. I probably should have had they bothered to call, but my ire on the way this case was handled, steadied at a rolling boil.

I had an entire surly speech prepared for the oral argument on reopening the Article 32(b) preliminary hearing. Fortunately, or maybe unfortunately, the judge raised his hand to stop me from speaking. Not in a dismissive way, but more in an "I've got you," expression. He unleashed on the government counsel there before him. Truth, the American way, and a simple sense of fairness were raised. Judge Aaron Rugh appropriately shamed the trial counsel and did not give him much of an opportunity to defend their ludicrous position that the first hearing had satisfied even basic process.

Most of the motions I had filed could wait for ruling until we conducted the actual Article 32(b). The judge deferred ruling on those, but he granted the classified discovery. The government would be required to produce the nuclear capability report that President Obama received. He also granted the new hearing.

The second preliminary hearing was presided over by a senior Navy CAPT who had been activated from the reserve component for the sole purpose of presiding over this prelim. The hearing would last three days in San Diego.

Among other witnesses, the defense called a retired Combatant Commander to explain the conspiracy. Let me say that again, we called to the stand to attest under oath about the grand conspiracy that actually transpired, and the source for this information was a retired Combatant Commander. That's, as they say, a big deal.

The trial counsel present did not comprehend the significance of what was being attested to, and it was almost like shooting fish in a barrel. The hearing officer nervously looked around when I announced we would be calling Admiral Cecil Haney and of our desire to call Admiral Dell Bull. Admiral Bull would essentially voluntarily absent himself from participating in the hearing. Avoiding perjury is a strong motivation.

Admiral Bull had been the one to communicate the threat to Heather to change her report or else. He had denied the conversation during our prehearing interview. Funny thing, we had ample evidence that it had taken place exactly the way Heather had recounted it to multiple senior leaders.

It was hard to tell if those in this conspiracy had appreciated that we would shine a giant brilliant headlamp of light onto the truth of Heather's experience. They were fools to think otherwise.

Heather Cole is the most honorable, candid, and strongest beacon for transparency I have ever known. She has worked on projects that are beyond any security clearance I could ever hope to achieve. And despite the torture the Navy tried to inflict on her, she remained a humble faithful servant. At every decision point in airing the Navy's dirty laundry, her first inclination was not to. Only with intention and my assurance we would only reveal the bare minimum, was I given greenlights to unearth more.

The Article 32(b) preliminary hearing officer's report concluded that there was no probable cause that Heather had committed any offenses and recommended dismissal of all charges. Then, the government actually complied and dismissed. We naively thought the nightmare was over. Oh no. Silly us.

They transferred the matter to another command and pursued a Board of Inquiry to make Heather show cause for her retention in the Navy after nearly thirty years of dedicated and impeccable service. They were trying to take her retirement.

Did I mention that we were months into the world shutting down due to COVID-19 by this point? And we were fast approaching Heather's mandatory retirement date.

Note: The military cannot hold a person past mandatory retirement date to pursue administrative actions like a board.

Commercial airline flights were being cancelled left and right, and eventually the Navy would deny me the ability to be present with Heather for the board. The Navy refused to allow us to appear in front of the board at all, except over a Zoom® type platform that kept failing. The three admirals presiding over the board were each in separate geographical locations on the east coast, Heather was stuck in a SKIFF on Tinker Air Force Base, I was relegated to a board room on board Naval Base Kitsap in Bremerton, Washington and the new, exceptional, and by-name requested detailed military counsel was made to stay in San Diego.

Heather's placement in the SKIFF meant that she could not have a personal cell phone to communicate with her lawyers. She was given a government landline to use, if needed. Right. Because we totally trusted the government phone. In a case where powerful instruments of the US military were trying their hardest to silence us all.

During the board, the bridge connecting us to the three admirals serving as the board members crashed multiple times. It even froze during my closing argument. The board president asked me to back up a few sentences. Unlike the government counsel who was reading their closing from a typed statement, I was not. Extemporaneous speaking and all. I did my best to back up a few sentences.

This was my first foray into trying to advocate across a screen. I didn't care for it much.

At the board's conclusion, they determined almost all of the misconduct had been unsubstantiated. I am still confused how they concluded she misused Navy aircraft. Nevertheless, she was retained, which means her retirement was intact. Admiral Haney had essentially threatened the board members personally if they did not get to the right answer. No, really.

You might think this was the end of the chapter of Heather's story. Oh no, you would be wrong.

Next up, the Navy's attempt to administratively reduce Heather by several grades, to the rank at which they alleged she had "last honorably served." Our only recourse is to provide a written response. We solicited letters of support that Heather should be allowed to retire as a Navy Captain.

I am proud to say that Heather is post-service, retired at the right grade of O-6. When we first met over the phone years before, she had already turned down Admiral.

When her case ended, I sent all of the information to the reporter for the Navy Times who had been a willing instrument for Heather's character assassination. I wanted to see something in print to set the record straight. It would never come.

I hope that providing the information I have in this book, that it will spark an investigation against the conspirators, and even ignite some righteous Congressional hearings. Our nation is less safe without Heather Cole's courage of conviction. And I doubt very seriously the issues that Heather attempted to bring out in her report have been addressed. I remain humbled she chose me to serve as her champion and advocate.

As I sat in that cold car on Joint Base Elmendorf-Richardson, Alaska years before the conclusion of her case, I was trying to make sense of her initial call. I asked her whether I could find out how it was that she found me. "No, you may not" was her response.

I still don't know exactly how she found me, but I do know the why. And I feel inspired to have fought the battle with and alongside of her.

Chapter 3

BREAKING "RULES"

I said no to him. A lot.

I had drawn a seemingly immovable boundary against defending child sexual abuse allegations as a civilian court-martial practitioner. When I began my private practice in 2012, I had been prosecuting very egregious cases of the same genre, even setting records for achieving life without parole sentences in non-homicide trials.

The pressure of those cases was not something I was looking to repeat. In fact, signing up for it seemed nearly impossible. When I announced my exodus from active duty, my boss, the Chief of the Trial Counsel Assistance Program, asked me to consider staying in position as a Special Victim Prosecutor for a third year.

My immediate guttural response to him was "do you want me to lose my soul?" And I definitely meant it.

There is nothing I have encountered in almost two decades of practice that is more taxing than to cultivate a relationship with a sexually abused child, to obtain their trust, and then to exact from them the details of their abuse in a public forum with their abuser sitting and watching them. Nothing.

It seems the universe said I was ready before I knew that I was. Thank heaven Sergeant First Class Sanchez and I found each other.

He was persistent in securing my representation. Becoming his fan and close friend was a lovely bonus. Whenever we reconnect over the years, he still calls me his "guardian angel." I'd never imagined or asked for this title, but I feel at ease when he says it. I receive it.

At the outset and while he was pursuing my legal defense, he never wavered; he insisted he was innocent. Candidly, that does little to sway me in taking a case.

Many believe that lawyers will only fight hard for a client they deem factually innocent. Perhaps those lawyers exist. That is not me, and never has been. Plus, almost everyone professes their innocence. At least at first.

This perspective client convinced me that I should at least view the forensic interview of his accuser. Or maybe that was my concession. That specific detail is not one I have retained. But I vividly recall sitting at the conference table at the Trial Defense Service office on Joint Base Lewis-McChord opposite the screen that would play the interview. The senior defense counsel, Major Donel Davis, was there acting as Vanna White.

About twenty minutes into the interview, I turned to Sergeant First Class Sanchez, and I said, "You didn't do this." His immediate reply through a nervous laugh of sorts: "That's what I've been trying to tell you."

He was smiling but also was profanely serious. A twinge of nervous energy to it, but some relief that I conveyed belief. Yeah, I replied. That's what everyone says.

I explained to him and to Major Davis that not only could I tell the teenage accuser was lying, but also the forensic interviewer could as well. Or at least the interviewer had strong suspicions. It's all in the questions. The framing, the cadence. Plus, every time the accuser was prompted for a natural detail, she responded to the question by repeating it. Never a good sign for credibility. Guarded and looking for more time before answering. The stalling would repeat in substantial measure during the trial.

I agreed to take his case. The need I had to solve the puzzle had begun.

I would come to learn that he had raised his accuser since she was only a few months old, dating the girl's mother, and eventually marrying her mom. Sergeant Sanchez and his spouse would go on to have two children together, and though he always felt like they had three children, his accuser harbored a different perspective.

One of the most difficult challenges in the case was the circumstance of how the disclosure was made. By first appearance, the outcry came as part of a suicide attempt by the teenager. In the defense world, we call that a "bad fact."

As we dug into the case, it revealed itself as contrived and not genuine. But proving that wouldn't be easy.

The "suicide" note was staged, placed in a location that would seem unlikely to be recovered, but she was cunning. On the back of the note there were hash marks to signify the number of ibuprofen the accuser said that she took as part of her suicide attempt.

It just so happened that the exact number of ibuprofen tick marks she recorded is precisely what Google® will tell you is the number that a person needs to take in order to die. Yeah. Seriously.

Only problem with this part of her story was that had she in fact taken this number of ibuprofen it would have shown in the labs that were drawn at the hospital. You guessed it; nothing indicated she had taken any. There would have been impacts to her kidneys and other vital organs. The lab results confirmed she was lying. We called the Emergency Room doc to testify at trial.

Did military law enforcement bother to check on this or any aspect of the accuser's story? Of course not. Don't be silly. Remember that from the highest brass, the message rings loud and clear: keep the alleged victim happy. Seriously.

One of the many decisions a trial lawyer makes is whether to prepare and recommend that the client takes the stand. I could spout off to you chapter and verse about the fact that a jury, and even a military panel, is not to hold it against the accused person if he does not testify. But that would be what we call textbook law.

The jury, or as we call it the court-martial panel in the military, is told that they are not to take silence by the defendant into consideration. But they do. I know they do. Particularly if the military accused is a senior enlisted or an officer.

I knew that in order to commit to winning, Sergeant Sanchez would probably need to testify. I encourage all defense counsel to prepare their client for testimony. When you make a battle plan, you want to make sure you have all possible weapons available. Perhaps during the battle, you realize you don't need your field artillery. But why would you ever not have them ready? I see a parallel for the accused's potential testimony. Have it ready. Every time.

My client and later friend had at this point in his career served nearly two decades in the Army. I suspect that he was raised to value strength and self-sufficiency. As a man who was suffering the trauma of having his own daughter accuse him of these most heinous acts, Sergeant Sanchez had palpable defensive walls.

In the world of criminal charges, appearing defensive means you look like you have something to hide, and therefore, you appear guilty. A defensive posture is poison to testimony.

When it was time to gear up again for Sergeant Sanchez's trial, I had fairly recently returned from a trip to the Trial Lawyer's College®, which had been held at that time at Gerry Spence's Thunderhead Ranch. One of the gems I took from this month-long training was using psychodramatic tools to discover the story. This often means reflecting and then reversing roles with a person to understand their truth, their feelings, and by extension, their motivations.

I met my client in my Tacoma office and told him we had some work to do on his direct. Arms crossed; he sat opposite me. I asked if he trusted me. There's that slightly nervous laugh again. Of course, he said. He was paying me a hefty sum of money as proof.

Not satisfied with the surface answer, I looked at him carefully and asked whether he truly trusted me. He met my gaze and assured me that he did. That he did not trust anyone else. And I believed him.

By the time of trial this man had been my client for nearly four years, and in that time, I created a safe space for him to not be okay about what was happening TO him.

In my office that afternoon, I explained that under the military's rules and statutes, I would likely never have an opportunity to interview his accuser before I would face her for cross-examination at trial.

Can we just take a moment for that fact? That before any military trial, I will almost never be afforded a chance to interview the central witness. Civil attorneys are always shocked to learn this. What about the discovery tool of depositions, they ask? Those are few and far between, and I know of one military appellate case where a judge's order for an alleged victim to finish answering Article 32(b) questions in a deposition was upheld. During my career, I also won a motion to compel the alleged victim in a case to submit to a defense psychiatric interview or else she would be precluded from testifying in the trial. Those cases are rare. And typically, my first time speaking to an alleged victim happens during cross-examination at trial.

I explained to Sergeant Sanchez that he knew his accuser, had lived with her for nearly 17 years, and he knew her in a way that I could not. He insisted that he clearly did not know her for her to levy these allegations against him. I insisted he did.

I explained that I wanted him to reverse role with his accuser, step into her actual role, and then answer my questions as though he were his accuser. In the first person. A nervous chuckle. It probably seemed silly. But he trusted me, so we began.

In the first few questions, there was push back. He would either answer in the third person or step into his own role and say, "I have no idea how SHE would answer." We got there eventually, this time as I persisted.

As his accuser, (s)he recounted growing up in a household where (s)he did not feel she belonged. I watched the walls melt away from his heart. And then we struck gold. As his accuser, Sergeant Sanchez shared with me a story he had not thought of in years. He recounted to me how in a moment of anger, he and his wife, her mother, had taken away his accuser's sense of belonging.

I won't share the exact detail because it is too deeply personal. It shook both of us. And then we both understood how she could turn on him in this way, so much pain that she carried. He wept. I believed him when he said he had not cried since he was a small boy.

Understanding, deep appreciation, and a somber acknowledgment enveloped his spirit. The defensiveness was gone, having melted away. Thank you, psychodrama.

Even though this had been my hope: to gain some insight into her motivation, I was not prepared for what we would learn. The process was transformative for him, but also for me. I was ready to make the Kool-Aid® in support of using psychodramatic tools in litigation, not just drink it.

The prosecutors insisted on calling to testify a group of girls the alleged victim knew growing up to ask about the accuser's outcries to them. I dubbed them "the teenager parade." The accuser had recounted many different versions of her alleged abuse. The gaping chasm of differences would make them fruitful witnesses for the defense. With each turn and twist, and variation, the panel grew more and more skeptical.

Government counsels' desire to win more than they cared to do justice was pronounced. In criminal litigation, I often find that a jury will align itself with the side who is the harbinger for the truth. Generally, jurors don't like when lawyers get in the way of information coming to their attention. If a trial advocate can create a circumstance when the government seeks to stop evidence the advocate knows is admissible and will be admitted, the defense inevitably will gain allegiance from one or more panel members.

I highlighted the prosecutor's desire to keep valid information away from the panel and their accordant desire to win over doing justice through the carefully orchestrated cross-examination of the prosecution's expert in child forensic psychology.

One of the more troubling tactics the government had taken in this case was to ignore the substantial evidence that undermined the accuser's credibility. I am not just addressing their failure to fully investigate; I mean to highlight that in the ramp up to the third trial date – yes, you read that or in the case of the audiobook, heard that correctly – the prosecutors reviewed the evidence we had marked for trial.

This evidence included military orders, parenting plans, plane tickets, and the like to indicate that for three of the charged timeframes, Sergeant First Class Sanchez and his accuser were not in the same geographical location.

Instead of surveying this alibi defense with the correct lens of skepticism writ large of the accuser's credibility, the prosecutors thought they would make this evidence irrelevant by dismissing only the affected charges. We learned they would be taking the recommendation for this partial withdrawal and dismissal to the convening authority. I wrote a 12 page document outlining why the correct and just action would be to withdraw and dismiss the entire case. You are shocked that they did not take my recommendation.

The government counsel apparently believed that the dismissed offenses and the underlying evidence no longer served any purpose in the trial. They were wrong. In my intentional and strategic interview of the government's expert, which I uncharacteristically took after the direct examination was completed, I followed through on my plan.

You see, when a witness is interviewed after their direct examination and before cross-examination, the witness is not permitted to speak to the counsel who called them to testify on direct. Not until their examination is completed. I strongly suspected the government had informed their expert about our evidence exonerating Sergeant Sanchez of many of the previously charged offenses. If that were the case, then the next piece would be to solicit if that knowledge impacted her expert opinion. Cha-ching. The payout could be immense.

During the brief interview (I didn't really need to interview her – I had my cross-examination already drawn up), the government's expert confirmed that the prosecutors had fallen into the ravine. Yes, she knew about the exonerating alibi evidence that confirmed the defendant and his accuser were not on the same continent or in the same state during much of the alleged misconduct. And yes, this evidence impacted her opinion. Thanks. That will be all.

The best part was the expert could not warn the prosecutors about what was coming. She cannot speak to the prosecuting attorneys while she is in the midst of testifying. Which of course I knew and factored into my strategy. Experience matters.

The expert resumes her seat on the stand, and I take her through the planned cross-examination. No big surprises, but still undercutting her testimony.

Then, I ask whether she was aware of allegations by the accuser against Sergeant Sanchez that were not before the members. Objection! From the prosecution table. Lead counsel requests and receives an Article 39(a) session.

An Article 39(a) session is the military's equivalent of a sidebar. Every word spoken in a court-martial is captured on the record. If words need to be spoken outside the presence of the panel, the military jurors are excused so that the counsel can speak openly and plainly about evidentiary issues without the risk of tainting the jurors from hearing the discussion.

After the jury is escorted by a bailiff back to their deliberation room to await the judge's determination on the objection, I explain that the expert witness confirmed to me that she was aware of the allegations that were not on the charge sheet, that she was aware of the evidence that contradicted those allegations, and that this knowledge had impacted her opinion.

The prosecutor's eyes grew wide, as he started to see he was not avoiding this evidence coming in front of the members. As I often do, I tossed out the concession that I did not intend at all to insert the additional fact that Sergeant First Class Sanchez had once been charged with these other allegations or that those allegations alone had been dismissed by the convening authority.

I was reassuring the judge that I knew the "inside baseball" as we sometimes call it, was not fair game or appropriate for the panel's consideration. The lead prosecutor, while lamenting what he saw as having been outflanked, conceded that he would withdraw his objection based on my acquiescence to not include the previous charging and dismissal. The questions and their answers would come in.

As the panel filed back in, I saw many faces eagerly awaiting resolution of this issue. When the questions were permitted and the answers came, I looked to the faces of the panel members. They learned that the accuser had made substantial allegations that could not be true because she was not collocated with Sergeant Sanchez for any of them.

I could sense that many members had come over to the support of the defense. Before this moment, I had a sense that at least two members were with us. But there was an astute acknowledgment of the significance of this alibi evidence and also a somber reflection of the heavy burden that had nearly flattened my client over the span of four years.

He, and countless others, were made to suffer under the weight of baseless charges, wrought with shame and disgust.

Field artillery engaged. Sergeant First Class Sanchez testified. He was compelling. Even without the missteps of the accuser.

At one point during my cross-examination of her, cornered with nowhere to go, she paused and stared around the room for more than thirty seconds. I let it go for that long, but I could not let it go longer. She knew her lies were being exposed, and she knew everyone in the room knew it also. But I could not be cruel, lest I risk allowing the members to shift in their allegiance away from the defense, wanting to align with her as a wounded person. So, I moved on. The point had been well made.

During panel member selection, there had been one female major who I knew bore a bias against my client. I had the opportunity to use a peremptory "just because" challenge after the judge denied our very close call challenge for cause. Had we used the peremptory, we would have needed to go through selection with a pool of additional members who I did not know anything about.

Sometimes, as the saying goes, the devil you know is better than the devil you do not.

On a military jury, the senior by rank person is the president of the panel. But as a trial advocate, you must also factor in group dynamics. Considering personality, position, station in life, the words a person uses in answering a question, the non-verbal cues, and countless other factors, is crucial.

Even though the panel president would be a senior officer, I was confident that two senior enlisted members would serve as my de facto co-presidents in the deliberation room, and that their collective voices would echo far louder and with greater influence than hers.

I was right.

There may be a place in the courthouse where a bystander can hear muffled screams from the deliberation room. If there are any. Not words, mind you, and not discussion, and most certainly not secret written balloted votes or opinions. But perhaps the tones of strongly held reverberating beliefs.

It may also be that during the deliberations in this case, two male voices could be heard battling against a sole female voice. I was right. They held their own and fought back against her tirade.

We "won."

Does anyone really win in cases like these?

Sergeant Sanchez was acquitted. And I know he would still rather have been accused of murder. He told me so. And I believed him.

The few who watched this two-week long trial know it was not merely that the government failed in its burden, but rather that Sergeant First Class Sanchez is a factually innocent man.

Forever changed by the "system" that cast him aside despite the heroism he showed in combat. But ever humble, he did not share his bravery with me. I had to learn about it from a fellow warrior.

Persistence paid off. Him in seeking my aid, and me in chiseling away at his walls. His persistence also melted my ice cold barrier against taking these emotionally taxing cases.

I wear the "Sanchez" necklace most often when I cross-examine an accuser. I usually text him to tell him so. He dutifully responds, and always tells me how nice it is to hear from his "guardian angel."

I am honored to also count him as my friend.

Chapter 4

RIPPLE EFFECTS

I responded to his web-based request for consult in what I imagine was a record-setting time. His judge advocate legal advisor convinced him that the trajectory of his suspension from command was not in his favor; he would need independent counsel.

When asked who his jag would recommend, he came up with only one name: mine. You probably saw that one coming. I'll try to do better and add some noteworthy cliffhangers. TikTok® is perhaps an easier platform for it.

Colonel Ralph Overland was commander for the 3d Armored Cavalry Regiment, Fort Hood, Texas. His name would become intertwined with the tragic end of Specialist Vanessa Guillen. Ralph was her regimental – think Brigade level – commander.

Though he has commanded and supervised many, his responsibility for her as one of his troops would be his legacy. I feel deeply committed to ensuring that his legacy is one that is accurate.

Plainly, the media did not get it right, neither did Secretary of the Army, and not even close was the account portrayed in the Netflix® "documentary" *I am Vanessa Guillen*. Not by a longshot.

Ralph has presence. That much was clear from our first phone call. His ability to lead and to engender faith is unparalleled in my modest estimation. While he knows who he is, as do countless others with whom and for whom he has served, I wish for others to also.

No matter how he found me, whether it was by referral, Google® search, or TikTok's algorithm, I know our paths were fated to intersect. Ralph Overland explained to me that he certainly wanted to correct the record regarding any missteps the public had been made to believe he had made, but more importantly, he wanted to improve the system.

Let's just let that sink in please. Colonel Overland cared about changing policy and helping those whose paths might follow his. My response? Have you come to the right advocate!

Anyone who has followed my blog for any amount of time at all, knows that I have been shouting from the rooftop about all manner of changes I want to make to a system that fails its people daily. And I don't just mean those accused; I mean survivors too. I am a proud instigator, someone who represents the voice of those who have been stifled and without meaningful opportunity for influence.

Ralph hired me to answer what we knew was coming: derogatory findings as part of an Army Regulation 15-6 investigation into the disappearance and death surrounding Vanessa Guillen's tragic end. I remember receiving the numerous subparts of the redacted investigation on the day before Christmas Eve 2020. In total, the investigation spanned more than twelve hundred pages. We had been simultaneously served the Fort Hood Independent Review Committee's conclusions, a modest one hundred thirty-six pages. Our suspense? The notification portended two weeks. Seriously? Seriously.

I requested two additional months. The government settled on giving me one month, two weeks past the original two-week suspense.

I was in a cabin near Cle Elum with my four children. I mom'd hard during the day and until bedtime, and then set out to analyze the findings in Ralph's investigation. I worked from 10pm until about 2:30am each night over this winter "break." Restless sleep until about 7am. Lather, rinse, repeat.

The fragmented investigation averred three discrete derogatory findings against Colonel Overland. They were that he and his Command Sergeant Major failed to take reasonable and appropriate measures to verify compliance with Task Force Phantom and Fort Hood's COVID-19 "shelter in place" guidance; that Colonel Overland allowed a gap in communication with Specialist Guillen's family that was too long and created a void in command messaging; and that Colonel Overland and the company level commander – prior to the focus on Specialist Guillen's case – were not sufficiently involved in the 3d ACR Sexual Harassment and Assault Response Program (SHARP).

What I believe we conveyed best as we dismantled each of the three findings was that the horrific tragedy that Vanessa was killed did not mean that any one act or a multitude of acts could have prevented it.

Sadly.

One of the curses and blessings of the military is its willingness to review its own conduct with a rather discerning and even dissecting eye.

What is deeply regrettable is the idea that because something terrible happened, there necessarily could have been actions taken to prevent it. And moreover, that someone should be identified as blame worthy. Someone other than her murderer.

No matter what procedures had been in place, if someone wanted to act against Specialist Guillen and harm her, that's precisely what would happen. That provides little comfort to her family, to those who loved her, and for anyone who watched the calamity unfold in the press, some even with worry about their own sons and daughters.

The Trial Defense Service detailed two attorneys to assist in Colonel Overland's defense. One was the Regional Defense Counsel, Lieutenant Colonel Lawrence Steele, and a captain from his office, Cody Steen. I have known Lawrence since we served as captains moons ago. He is a good man, and he served as a helpful sounding board and repository for my many drafts in response. An even more integral member of the team was Cody Steen.

The team worked rather frenetically but systematically. One of the vulnerabilities of the scope of the investigation was that the investigators had divvied up responsibility for different aspects of liability. I recognized why this approach seemed best given the breadth of what they were examining, and in managing any large project, this often makes sense. And both Lawrence and particularly Cody were peppering me with offers to help. My approach to any puzzle analysis has always been and I imagine will remain is to work independently before collaborating.

I asked them to each do their own dive into the three derogatory findings. We would come together once I had created my own draft. I have found that if I were to read someone else's notes or draft, it could foreclose on the creativity of my process, perhaps even limiting me from seeing an issue I would otherwise have recognized.

Once I developed a draft to one derogatory finding, I would send it to the team. They would review, edit, and send back to me. We were working in tandem, and it proved effective.

I did not want to issue any drafts for Colonel Overland's review until I had edited the version that came back from the team, ruminated over it on my own, and then really refined these subparts. Then I would send them to the team for additional feedback, await their notes, edit myself again, before providing anything to Ralph.

I worked on responding to each derogatory finding in a separate document, refined each, and then sent back and forth to the team, before settling down on any specific arguments.

Recall that I also worked at night after my kids went to sleep. Then I would rest for about 4 hours, wake up early before my kids did, and start the process all over again. All told, I had to read almost two thousand pages, many times over. I digested them, rolled them over in my mouth like a Cabernet Franc… until I felt like I could have something to say.

As I mentioned, the investigation had been put together by multiple different assistant investigating officers…very poorly, like poor patchwork from a disjointed team – can we call it a team? – who were not even internally consistent in their findings. We identified those conflicts, highlighted their inconsistency, and used them to great success.

One of the many reasons that I admire Colonel Ralph Overland as much as I do is that while he certainly wanted to refute the derogatory findings that had been levied against him, he emphasized to me early in our attorney-client relationship that he wanted to do more. He wanted to improve whatever we could; he knew we had a senior audience who could effectuate change. In particular, he wanted to examine what organizational requirements communicate to Troopers and leaders; he also wanted to note the limitations of and to improve those instruments being used to evaluate learning, and significantly, to rework systems to help avoid attrition to ensure Troopers feel connected and valued. What does that have to do with the death of a female Soldier? Everything, I assure you.

I am vastly proud of much of the writing that we produced on Ralph's behalf, and not because it was well phrased, although it was. One of my favorite passages speaks to one of the most significant pitfalls of any system or organization:

...complacency is the hallmark of an organization that stretches its members past its emotional limits. We grow complacent because we are inundated with being told to care about too many requirements. With the benefit of hindsight, I can say that I wish that I would have better evaluated where the numbers do not presently reach: the requirements to ensure people feel valued. The years of "Winning Matters," "Mission First," and an over-reliance on numbers and deployment readiness statistics have muddied the path for how to accomplish the mission while taking care of our people.

One of the challenges we faced was supposed "data" that Soldiers did not know the basics of Sexual Harassment and Assault Response Program (SHARP); namely, the "data" showed that Soldiers did not know how to report a SHARP incident. It was critical to understand why this data could not be accurate. We explained:

> As anyone who has spent time with Troopers can attest, there has to be a reason for the Trooper to care about the instrument. Without their buy in, the tool is another use of their time they may even see as a waste. Whether they mistrust what the feedback will give them, or they patently think the time when the questions were asked came too late, I remain skeptical that the survey provided the data it sought.

We described instead that wherever "checks on learning" were going to be used, they needed to demonstrate to the Soldier that their time and responses matter. We reminded our audience about the pre-tests on some annual requirements that inevitably produce the most careful and accurate responses of all military training. We juxtaposed how the Army trains SHARP differently from any other facet of military preparedness.

In small group learning environments on SHARP, I proposed to let Troopers know at the outset there will be an individual test at the end, that for those Troopers who demonstrate a grasp of the information, they will not have to repeat training. We use parallel methods in nearly all other aspect of military learning. "Training to standard, not to time" has been a mantra and model for decades, yet this is the opposite of how we have trained SHARP. The Troopers get the message that SHARP standard is: Were all the warm bodies present for training; and that if they were, that was enough. If we trained using the same method in any other facet of Army training, people would be dying. It is frankly shocking that we are surprised by the statistics we see about learning SHARP policies given how we train. Especially in this arena where commanders are being held to a standard for their Troopers' learning, it is necessary that we develop instruments that accurately reflect what we are trying to measure.

Colonel Overland knew there were deficiencies and he wanted to effectuate change, or at least to use this platform as an opportunity to be part of the dialogue. He gave me the chance to put into one memorandum what I have been spouting on my website's blogpost for more than a decade. As a senior leader, he recognized that because of my experience as a military magistrate, command legal advisor, trial counsel, defense attorney, and special victim prosecutor that my perspective was unique. He valued my insight. This is leadership. He recognized that there was deficiency, but he also knew that he did not know precisely how to fix it. So, he sought out a trusted advisor who did. And then he evaluated my ideas, we refined them together, and we proposed workable solutions. We wrote:

> I have gleaned in this process the way to permeate the necessary shift in culture is through hands on approach to leader development. As we move beyond a checklist for conveying command teams' responsibilities, we need to rework fundamentals of command, and to live and demonstrate the tenant of showing dignity and respect. One of the ways we can begin to scratch the surface of showing true caring is to not do what is already happening: developing a policy to then push down to the Troop level. We need to develop the policy by asking the Troopers what they believe the policy should be: we need their feedback, we need to know how these policies impact them, and we need their buy-in. We should not ignore the blunders of our past to cause us to rush through developing more "solutions." The reality is that if we push down another policy without their input, what will be inherent in the policy is mistrust and a sense that they do not matter. They

will already believe that this is yet another way that some egghead theorist on Capitol Hill is telling them how it is, rather than anyone bothering to ask them what it should be. We will lose again before we start.

Within forty-eight hours of our submission of Colonel Ralph Overland's response, U.S. Armed Forces Command (FORSCOM) implemented our proposals. And then FORSCOM pushed them up to the Department of the Army.

Ralph Overland is a leader who cares, and every organization with whom he worked, for whom he worked, or which he led was bettered by his proximity and leadership. I'll never forget when Ralph told me he wanted to shape SHARP policy in his response matters. I replied, "Sir, have you come to the right lawyer."

I could not be prouder to have stood up for him, against odds that seemed impossible. Not only did we defeat each of the three derogatory findings, but also Colonel Overland was the only commander at Fort Hood to do so surrounding the tragedy of Specialist Guillen's murder. Beyond this superlative was my infinite honor to have used the platform to position us to effectuate real and discernible change.

Jocelyn C. Stewart

Chapter 5

POKE TO THE STOMACH

My husband *at the time...* don't get all excited... approached me in my office in the middle of the afternoon and told me there was a case he wanted to pull me onto. He explained that he had what he thought was a no bullshit, factually innocent client. In a moment of rare vulnerability, he was not sure whether he could do the case justice alone.

We were both serving as uniformed defense counsel at what was then called Fort Hood Texas. I had been a prosecutor for more than two years before doing another year as a defense counsel in Germany. My then spouse had not prosecuted or defended prior to this first assignment as a military defense attorney.

In approaching me, he explained that he wanted to ask permission for our boss, the senior defense counsel, at Fort Hood to assign me to represent the common client. To make him the client of a married couple. What could possibly go wrong?

Plenty was going wrong in the marriage apart from the case. But it would be almost a decade before I would be strong enough to leave him. By appearances, we were a couple who could withstand the challenge of a joint representation. And we did.

There were some interesting dynamics during trial prep and even during the trial, which I'll get to soon enough. When we asked (then) Major Daniel Everett whether I could join the defense team for this case, he barked. It's kind of his way. Did he need to be concerned this case would make us divorce? We assured him it would not.

Dan's decision to allow us to try the case together was the right call. For the client and the case.

Our client was charged with Aggravated Assault with a dangerous weapon for allegedly stabbing his estranged girlfriend in the abdomen, and another specification of assault consummated by a battery over a period of time that alleged an abusive romantic relationship. Lastly, there was an allegation the client had violated a military protective order by having contact with the accuser at a party one weekend.

None of it happened. Well, none of the assaulting happened. And the violation of the order would get dismissed before the jury could consider it in their deliberations. (Insert best sinister laugh.)

We gave alibi notice in the case that our client was asleep in his barracks room when the alleged victim claimed that she had been stabbed. At the other end of a very large barracks on the installation.

The alleged victim had been telling her female first sergeant that she was in an abusive relationship with our client. A first sergeant is the senior enlisted person in a company, who advises the company commander, and ensures the non-commissioned officers are meeting and exceeding standards as leaders for the Soldiers of the company.

As a result of the accuser's story to her first sergeant, our client received an order to not come within so many feet of his accuser. Meanwhile, the alleged victim is telling our client she does not understand where the command had the idea that the client was abusing her. She claims that it must have been a third party intervener giving the chain of command the wrong impression.

Client tells his accuser that he is going to abide by the order and that she needs to also.

One night, the client is awakened by pounding on his barracks door. After he sleepily staggers to the door, he opens it and sees his estranged girlfriend and her roommate. The girlfriend tells him that an unknown man stabbed her in the stomach while she was walking down a barracks hallway. Even in his groggy fog, his first words are, "did you call the police? Call the police!" He finds his cell phone and offers it to her.

Her story evolved many times. The next version included that her unknown attacker was actually an "unknown black man." Seriously.

Then, when she was pulled aside by her female first sergeant, she "revealed" that what really had happened was that her estranged boyfriend, my client, had supposedly beaten her head against the side of the rough concrete walls of the exterior barracks stairwell several times before plunging a knife into her stomach, and then launching her down twelve concrete stairs.

The only injury on her was a 1 millimeter wide poke to her abdomen. A cotton swab blotted a solitary drop of blood. Seriously.

And the only knife recovered that night was in the jeans pocket of the complainant. Oops, I can't say "recovered" because that implies that law enforcement took it into their care and custody, which they did not. When I asked the officer why he didn't collect the knife from her at the hospital, his reply was that she told him that wasn't the knife her assailant had used.

She had two other knives in her barracks room also, by the way. Law enforcement did photograph those knives at least. The why would prove helpful.

This was the case that taught me that there is a distinct difference between sincerity and accuracy. In fact, this is the case for which I authored a series of *voir dire* questions that I continue to use when I am selecting a military court-martial panel. When the Article 32(b) occurred in this case, I believed the accuser. She was compelling. I met with the client after, and I laid into him like I was a drill sergeant. Seriously.

The client did not relent. He insisted he was innocent and that these events had never happened. I did not completely believe him when he denied wrongdoing. But I was duty bound to try to figure out a way to get to an acquittal.

Where did that leave me? I needed to sift through the evidence.

There is a not so nice expression for a defense that is not uncommon in criminal misconduct cases. It's called the "nutty-slutty" defense. It refers to casting aspersions at the complainant for being mentally unstable and for being promiscuous, and therefore untrustworthy.

When I turned to the puzzle of this case, I decided our "theory" needed to be that the accuser was mentally unstable. There was a part of me that still believed the client was merely convincing in his denials. I sat with that for quite a while and turned the idea over in my mind. What I finally realized was that the bias I brought to this case was that I did not want to live in a world where someone could be so convincing about an allegation and not be accurate. But that, my friends, is the precise reality in which we reside.

We obtained two forensic experts to assist in the defense of this case. I'll get to forensic psychiatry in a few paragraphs. But first, I want to start with the forensic pathologist we used.

I needed an expert in forensic pathology in this case to help me address the injury, or rather the lack of injury following her report of what she said transpired. For years, I have collaborated with Dr. Robert Bux, M.D. He was the elected coroner in El Paso County, Colorado for a long time. He retired fairly recently. The first time I worked a case that he was on was one of the Gangster Disciple cases out of Kaiserslautern, Germany; he was a defense expert, and I was the prosecutor. Any good expert can work a case from both sides of the aisle; Bob Bux is outstanding. I also count him as a friend.

In this case, Bob reviewed the complaining witness' account. He also reviewed the medical records from her trip to the emergency room after her initial report about the unknown assailant.

To assist him in explaining the injuries he would expect to encounter, Dr. Bux created a clear plastic overlay to present over the body diagram where the actual tiny injury had been documented. Bob drew on the clear sheet which injuries and their locations that he would have expected to see had the events actually transpired.

I am not someone who is particularly gifted at using courtroom technology, and this case dates back to about 2008. I am certain tech-savvy folks reading this account can think of a number of cool ways to present this evidence. But Bob's clear plastic sheet overlay was one of the most impactful methods I have seen or heard used in a courtroom presentation. As the panel members passed around the exhibit and flipped back and forth between the sole injury present on her abdomen and the plastic sheet of what should have been there, I watched the faces of each member react, process, and shift.

The military judge on this case was a Major at the time, and he would go on to become the Chief of the Army's Trial Judiciary. He told me during a session after the trial that I had won the case during *voir dire.*

Remember those questions about the difference between sincerity and accuracy? They were followed up with some questions about behavioral health. Sprinkle the seeds, hope a few land, watch them take root, and then grow into vines.

Voir dire was the seed sprinkling, and the plastic overlay was those seeds taking root.

Science gives people a reason to believe you. When you are the defense, there is always a skeptical and even hostile gaze at the outset of every trial. If you work hard to gain credibility, a shift happens. If you are a truth teller, military panels take note, and they will look to you for cues on how they should be responding to evidence. If you do your job.

It is important to acknowledge that we were unable to obtain Dr. Bux's assistance on this case initially. Under the military caselaw and the judge's ruling, we were entitled to an "adequate substitute" to the by name expert request we had made. The government instead appointed one or more experts from the US Armed Forces Medical Examiner's office (USAFME). Yeah, those guys did not work out so well.

When we used their assistance and the assistance of any appointed expert *consultant* it is protected by the same privilege to which attorneys and paralegals ascribe. As we discussed with these experts our theories for the injury as being self-inflicted, they denounced each one. It wasn't like I hadn't read scientific literature on the signs and symptoms of self-inflicted injuries. I politely tried to bring up data from these journal articles I had read. These clowns from USAFME were having none of it. It was staggering. During these frustrating meetings, they emphasized the dimensions of the wound as what they were really holding fast to as why our theory did not make sense.

But I had spoken to Bob Bux about the case, and he told me that he believed the emergency room (ER) physician had probably transposed the dimensions of the injury by depth and length. So, we went back to the ER doc, and he confirmed he had switched the numbers. Oops. Oy vey.

We alerted the Court that the USAFME experts were not accommodating our needs, and through a series of events, we convinced the judge to give us our by name expert.

During the trial, the prosecutor cross-examined Bob using the theories the USAFME experts had told us during our protected attorney-client discussions. I distinctly recall looking at my then spouse as he looked at me. His gaze conveyed that he felt like something untoward had taken place. I, dutifully giving everyone the benefit of the doubt, waved him off. It looked to me like the prosecutor had done her homework. Good for her, I thought.

Yeah. No.

After the trial, we found out that those USAFME experts had informed the government prosecutors on the case about everything they had told us. They all somehow thought since we weren't using them anymore, that meant they were fair game to educate the government.

I don't know how I can properly explain how many ethical rules and professional responsibility cannons this violated. Even recounting this transgression as I type or say it aloud makes my pulse soar and makes me want to scream. Make it make sense.

We found out the betrayal when the prosecutors inadvertently sent a draft USAFME "thank you" to a uniformed defense counsel in our office. Her last name was the same last name as a government paralegal.

She looked at the email and even though the case was over, thought it looked strange enough to pass along. Do you have any idea how lucky the government was that the trial resulted in a full acquittal? Oops – spoiler…

Let's move back to the forensic psychiatrist expert. On this case and so many others, I collaborated with Dr. Thomas Grieger, M.D. Sadly, the last time I reached out to work with him, I learned that he had suddenly and unexpectedly passed away.

Rest in Peace, Tom. You are missed.

We learned just prior to trial that the government had directed their forensic psychiatric expert to interview the complaining witness in the case.

At Tom's urging, I asked the military judge to compel an interview of the complainant by our expert. As part of the government's verbal response in the session, they cited to a case for the proposition that the military judge lacked the authority to compel a psychiatric evaluation of the complaining witness in a court-martial. I asked the military judge for an opportunity to review the case. I am so glad I did.

Government counsel have a way of only reading what are called "head notes" and often don't really account for what the totality of what the opinion is saying. This case was no different.

The military case law that this counsel cited to, gave significant support that in certain cases the military judge could in the interest of justice preclude a complainant from testifying if he or she did not submit to a defense psychiatric expert interview. This government counsel had literally provided the precise authority that I had spent an hour looking for but could not find. Thanks for your rushed preparation, my dear.

The military judge articulated detailed findings and stated that he agreed with the holding, which is the bottom line ruling of the case, that he could not compel her to submit to interview; but he also stated that under the facts of our case, that if she declined to submit to the defense psychiatric interview that he did have the authority to preclude her from testifying in front of the panel. Hot damn. He had stones. I mean, he probably still does. And his 2014 trial court ruling in *United States v. Major Michael F. Stellato* (aka, the banana in the box case) confirmed this position so many years later.

The accuser submitted to the defense expert interview and even a defense counsel interview. And she told each group different stories. Thirty minutes apart. Remember that theory she had mental health issues? Yeah, not a theory. Reality.

We strategically decided I would be "bad cop" during the defense interview of her, and that my then husband would be the "good cop" who would cross-examine her in front of the panel. She liked him. It was effective.

In a trial where your client is factually innocent, you never want to wonder if you should have deployed more of the weapons in your trial arsenal. I recall standing in response to the judge asking how many more witnesses the defense anticipated calling. My answer was 18. The panel members audibly groaned, after which I immediately changed my answer to "or 5."

The company level commander in this case had refused to swear to the charges. Even when the battalion commander tried to force her to. This company commander was deployed at the time of trial and had been the person to issue the no-contact order between my client and the alleging victim. This means the commander was a necessary witness in the trial. After some discovery violations by the prosecutors and the granting of a continuance as a result, I asked the judge to freeze the witness list and all discovery because I argued the government should not get to benefit from their own negligence. I meant malfeasance, but I was trying. The judge concurred.

The case continued for the eight weeks that I was out of the office, having given birth to my second child. During my maternity leave the prosecutors figured out their gap in witness list and asked the judge for leave of court to add "just one more witness." I learned this when my kids' dad came through the door to our home and handed me his laptop to read the government email. "They figured it out," he explained. I took control of the laptop and began typing out a terse reply. "No one is ever going to believe that I wrote that email," he quipped. I didn't care. We pressed send.

Within minutes, the military judge emailed us all a reply, declining to permit the government to add the commander to their witness list. Fist pumps to commemorate the government could not prove the one infraction our client had committed.

When the judge directed the panel to line through the charge related to the violation of the order, one of the more interactive panel members shook his head at the prosecutors in almost disgust and then turned to us with a smirk, as if to say, well done.

After the findings of not guilty were announced, our client's dad wept and thanked us profusely. Our client was grateful, but I could see he felt little vindication.

While I have not lived the experience as the accused person, having championed their causes for as long as I have, I imagine he is forever changed. I did not see any change in his affect at his acquittal; he looked almost stoic. He left the courtroom without many words.

I later learned that after the panel had all of the evidence and closed to deliberate but before coming out to announce their findings, that my client had approached the military judge to address him. As the judge was recounting this story to me, I know my pulse went through the roof. It is not kosher for the judge to speak with an accused outside of on-the-record required dialogue. The judge reassured me it was all fine.

Then he explained that my client had asked to shake his hand so he could thank him for ensuring he had had a fair trial. ((Heart swells)) Recall that this was before the verdict.

This Private First Class left the military as soon as his obligation was completed. He did not take solace in his acquittal, and he wanted nothing more to do with the Army who had turned their back on him. I hear this sentiment often.

In this case, he had been "awarded' through litigation with hundreds of days of credit toward any punishment of confinement because he had been made to live on a mattress at his supervisor's home. There is no way to cash that in when one is innocent. He wanted the Army in his rear view mirror.

We lost touch after he left the service. Wherever he is, I genuinely hope that he is healthy, well, and fulfilled. Heaven knows he deserves it.

Chapter 6

MEDICAL MOTIONS

When the rest of the world went to Zoom® court, the military said, "hold my beer."

I defended Colonel Daniel McKay for wildly false allegations of sexual assault in front of a panel of all general officers in the middle of the pandemic. For real.

The government flew in 18 general officers from across the Continental United States (CONUS) and even one from outside the Continental United States (OCONUS) in Alaska to sit on the venire as potential panel members. They also assigned a local one-star general from 7th Infantry Division to round out their numbers to 20.

Dan came to me originally because he was dealing with a notice related to his military medical credentials. He had received deficient legal advice from a uniformed defense counsel – I know you're shocked – and had accepted commanding general level nonjudicial punishment for events that either did not occur or which were grossly exaggerated, and none of which were criminal. This poor choice cascaded to a series of events that would lead to some of the most stressful times of Colonel McKay's life.

Less than a week after I met Dan in my office in downtown Tacoma, he received word that he was being targeted in an investigation for allegedly sexually assaulting... wait for it, the medical credentials manager at the hospital. You just can't make up this stuff.

If this were true, Colonel McKay would fall into the category of a special type of offender: one with particularly low impulse control. I mean, to assault the woman who is serving you with paperwork about your past allegations of inadvertently poking a colleague in the derriere with a pencil and encountering the tuchus – yes, it is a word... you can look it up – of a separate work colleague. That would be not only foolish but demonstrating grievously poor self-regulation, with little to no impulse control.

While it was important for me to consider the possibility that he was lying to me and that he really was guilty of all assertions, it wasn't long before I dismissed the notion completely.

Because of the poor advice of the military counsel, I was inheriting a case that meant more than an uphill battle. First, in addition to Dan accepting disposition at the nonjudicial punishment for his prior incidents, he pleaded guilty to them as actual assaults! Oh mercy. Second, the statement he issued as part of the plea apologized for his conduct. FML. Third, this meant that the government could seek and potentially prevail in introducing evidence of these prior incidents to obtain an explosive instruction for the military jury: that if they concluded the prior events occurred by a preponderance of evidence, they could use that to help them be convinced beyond a reasonable doubt of the charged incident. The instruction essentially calls the military defendant out as having a predisposition to commit this type of sexual misconduct. I just can't.

Thankfully, we didn't.

In the first wave of motions filed, I moved to exclude the prior events under Military Rule of Evidence 413 and Military Rule of Evidence 404(b). They are distinct, and their differences matter substantially.

Military Rule of Evidence 413 is a Congressional declaration that people who commit sexual offenses have a predisposition to recidivate and to repeat these kinds of offenses because that's just what they do and that's just who they are.

The instruction that a jury receives with this kind of evidence is so explosive that I am not aware of a defendant who has been found not guilty when this evidence and instruction comes into evidence. Not ever.

Military Rule of Evidence 404(b) is different, but still matters. The default rule in any criminal trial, whether civilian or military, is that all allegations must stand on their own and that evidence that a person committed a prior violation is not proof that the person committed the charged offense. This idea seems to most like legalese and creates a legal fiction that would seem to run afoul of common sense.

What do you mean, I can't decide that a person who did the same or similar thing on a previous occasion is more likely to have done it on the occasion when he is currently alleged to have done so? Freaking lawyers.

In the first motion I filed to keep these prior events out, I prevailed on two out of three of them. Sigh. Even one event coming into evidence and the accompanying judicial instruction had the high probability of burying Colonel McKay.

The greatest gift any judge can give to a litigator is their written opinion. Mine that shit for gold. And boy did I.

In reviewing the judge's written ruling, I realized the crack in the pavement. I went back and collected additional evidence to assist the judge in his required analysis. I obtained two more affidavits that struck exactly on what I could tell I had failed to connect for the judge in our first round of litigation. I filed a request to file a request for reconsideration out of time. After the judge granted it, I resubmitted it as part of a motion for reconsideration.

Let's take a pause for a moment for this idea that I have to file a request to file out of time before I can actually file the thing that I want to file out of time. Let's take another pause for a moment that there are some judges who have denied such requests to file out of time.

Before ever looking to whether the matter being filed on has any independent merits to it. Just "summarily denied." Seriously.

In this case, the judge was gracious and open to our filings. And not just what we call "pro forma" – for show or for appearances.

He dutifully is the kind of judge who wants to get it right. Were that all military accused would be so fortunate.

I know with specificity that this judge carefully reviewed our request for reconsideration. Mostly because we won. Boy, did we win. The ruling meant that no reference to any of the prior allegations would be admissible in Colonel McKay's trial, at least not during the prosecution's case.

In these kinds of battles, there are a number of ways that the prior alleged misconduct could become admissible during the trial. The litigator's job is to ensure that "door" never gets "opened." A win is only a win for so long as it remains a win. As I and others say, this is chess, not checkers.

This motions victory honestly changed the entire landscape of the trial. Without any hesitation, I can attest that this was the single most important reason for our victory. Spoiler alert – too late.

Well, I can say also that the alleged victim gets a major assist in our win. Her demeanor, delivery, and decorum were a substantial factor in why she would not be deemed credible.

Plus, she just wasn't actually credible. But details, right?

My esteemed colleague, Mr. Joshua Karton, says that as trial litigators we are the writer / actor / director of our own one-person play. As the lead counsel, in agreeing with Joshua, I likewise see my role as being there to weave the facts of a narrative that best supports my theory of the case. One of the scariest ways that this happens is when, as the storyteller, you know it isn't just a narrative, it isn't just a story.

When theater meets reality, and the person sitting next to you is factually innocent, the burden you experience to prove their innocence weighs mightily.

Back to the assist by the alleged victim. Before she entered the courtroom to approach the stand, we could all hear her coming. No, really.

She was wearing some device to assist her with breathing: a portable oxygen concentrator. It was noisy, and it made her look like a lunatic. Yes, I said that. And I truly mean it.

I recall vividly the military judge making eye contact with me, and his expressive eyes asking me "did you know about this??" and my eyes replying to convey most artfully, "no f'ing way, did I know about this."

I was teetering between anger that the prosecutors had not warned us and some level of stifled laughter. I mean, in viewing this moment like it was on a film, anyone reasonably watching would be in hysterics on their couch or even in one of those cozy reclinable chairs in a theater. But I don't get that "benefit" from the chair of lead counsel in a courtroom.

When you are a litigator, you are always on screen, always on the stage. Every micro-expression is being examined by everyone, though the group that matters most is the jury. And you just don't know how the others in the room are receiving the same information. The worst mistake any advocate can make is to presume their experience mirrors those of the persons who will sit in judgment. Any momentum is easily lost by giving a reason for the panel members to sympathize with the complainant.

Smirks, smiles, and laughs can be easily construed as bullying and cruel. While you can't and should not try to be a robot, you must always remain mindful that not everyone has your shared experiences.

This is particularly the case when it comes to the dark waters that trial litigators are baptized in and then bathe themselves in every time there's a new case. Jury members may only be compelled to drink a thimble of those dark waters.

As the complainant testified in between the clicks, exhales, and gasps of her device, at no point did she appear that she needed it. At least to me. My hope was that for as many of the panel members as possible, it would be like supplying the defense with our defense without needing to put a name on it.

Her story was already absurd. And it changed even more right before our very eyes.

I say, our eyes, because it is a shared journey that the trial litigator seeks.

A common theme that I fall back on is this idea of a shared experience for the defense and the jury where we are seeking the truth – not those people at the prosecutor's table. In doing so, we are aligning ourselves in a mission to free the client from the shackles of the false claims. The prosecution's oft myopathy and desire to win at all costs is their blinders, their kryptonite. F them. We, the defense, and the members of the jury, we, are on a shared path of uncovering truth.

I am at my core a truth teller. And that essential fact seems to run afoul of all understandings of anyone outside the system, with anyone who has an appreciation of the roles that people play in the process.

As a criminal defense attorney, I have proudly shroud myself in the black, dark hat of the bad guy. Everyone who works in the system thinks of the defense attorney as the bad guy, representing the bad guy. Think old western films.

Let's say that again: I wear the black hat proudly. But that isn't the role that wins cases. Who wants to align themselves with the bad guy? Not the flag waving, patriot juror. No, sir.

In my opening statement, I promised big when it came to the inconsistencies, the implausibility, and the internal irregularities of the complaining witness' future testimony. And I delivered.

One of the cardinal rules in trial litigation is never to over-promise in an opening statement about what you anticipate will come into evidence. You'd better damn well know the rules of evidence and procedure, anticipate objections, and understand where your judge will come down on decisions.

Bit by bit, you are building credibility with the panel. You know the evidence, you know the rules, and you are there to bring the panel on the journey you've already been on, searching for truth. Fail to deliver and you might as well hand over the verdict to the prosecution.

During my closing argument, I recall taking a chance and outright declaring that people senior to the prosecutors should have vetted the case better before flying 19 general officers in the middle of a pandemic. Three heads nod, returning my gaze in fixed solidarity. There's my acquittal. Oh yeah.

The panel returned findings of not guilty in an hour and ten minutes. Who's counting? I am. You betcha.

I went after the prosecutors with a furor in my closing, and it wasn't drama, not acting, or feigned fury.

There's a point when the absurdity of an allegation should penetrate the indignation of any prosecutor with the beaming light of truth.

It did not in this case, and my frustration erupts from me like GERD in a newborn. Even after a win, and particularly after a win.

In my career, I would say I have vacillated between clouds of quiet indignation and fiery eruptions of anger.

I recall a dear friend and colleague from whom I learned a great deal as a young prosecutor. He said, "conviction equals conviction." How profound. Indeed, if an advocate does not believe in what she is professing, why would anyone else?

The same rings true for any defense practitioner. A jury will see fear and guilt and worst of all shame in your eyes before you can take your chair if you do not believe in your client's cause.

Dan McKay is a good man. He also was not guilty of any of the prior misconduct events nor was he guilty of anything on his federal felony charge sheet.

He, like many, fell prey to believing in the system. Why would the appointed counsel not guide him to best decisions? Why would an investigation not sift through fact from fiction? How could anyone take the alleging victim's absurd allegations at face value? No, sir. Dan's case is yet another example of justice being for sale.

Despite my increased and waxing distaste for the military justice system, I remain incredibly humbled by that role that I get to play in it. Instigator, provocateur, and truth teller.

I am passionate about my role as the actual bearer of the western "white hat," no matter the type casting that tends to happen. Every trip into a courtroom starts off with this notion that defense attorneys are there to thwart justice. I am honored to be the one who in reality defends justice.

Our jurors, the last line of defense in an otherwise nearly indefensible system. And I am overwhelmingly proud to have been chosen to stand up for Dan.

Chapter 7

TINDER® TERROR

As far as I am concerned, she killed him.

It would not matter to me that he hanged himself in a barracks room on Joint Base Lewis-McChord. Not for one moment.

It would not matter to the world that he had been acquitted of a forcible rape by strangulation.

I won the case, but I lost Daniel. The world lost Daniel, and a substantial part of me will never get over it.

When I tallied the evidence and measured the odds early on, I saw us losing. And losing big. So, I did what I never do, and what I have vowed I won't do again: I asked the government for their best offer. That means, what would be the best deal they would offer my client if he pleaded guilty.

Anyone who knows me, or better, knows my reputation, knows that I don't go looking for plea deals. That's kind of who I am. I don't deal. And clients who find me aren't the people who are looking for deals.

The allegation was a forced rape by strangulation in the context of a Tinder® date gone wrong. That she owned her initial position (harr harr) of wanting sex from this stranger but explained that she revoked consent was what we call in this business, a bad fact. A really bad fact.

The photographs I had in discovery revealed apparent injury to her throat and neck.

A stranger rape with injury is the worst nightmare of a criminal defense attorney. So, in fear and from trepidation, I asked the government for their best offer. 7 years. That should have been my first clue there were issues in the case. It wasn't at first, but I would get there.

I was sitting in the living room of my then fiancé – Liz Taylor, much? It was in Kirkland, Washington. I took the call with Daniel to explain the precarious position that I saw him facing, and to recount the offer from the prosecution.

Through tears, my client told me that he could not plead guilty to something he had not done. There was a crack in his voice that spilled truth. I reassured him that I would not stop until I figured a way out of this for him.

Dangerous to make such a promise. And I am grateful that I found a way to deliver on it.

The lesson of that case was never to stop at the four corners of the government's "investigation." To do so is a huge mistake.

This was the case that I "took with me" to the Trial Lawyers College® when I made my voyage to Dubois, Wyoming. I carefully bubble wrapped its fragility in my psyche and placed it lovingly in my carryon. I needed to keep it close.

The experience that was the Trial Lawyers College® is its own book. For now, I'll explain that when I went there, it was three and a half weeks for litigators to experience hands on training. I thought it was finishing school for high level trial lawyers; turns out, not so much. At least not then. I hear tell that its rebirth post lawsuits, is more akin to what I was led to believe circa 2018 when I made my voyage there. Again, that is its own chronicle.

During one of our brief respites from training in Wyoming, I checked myself into a ridiculous suite in Hotel Jackson. I justified it because I had scheduled interviews on Daniel's case, including the alleged victim's current spouse. A business write-off at that. Plus, I needed the soothing that a certain thread count provides. Heavens to Murgatroyd was that trip to Jackson fruitful.

As we worked through the file, I noticed that military law enforcement had all but skirted around what I believe to be the most crucial interview in *any* sexual assault claim: the outcry witness.

There were two sentences in the report. No sworn statement, and no recorded interview. A mere two sentences that validated there had been contact between the accuser and her spouse. The accuser's recorded statement to law enforcement gave the impression of a middle of the night / 9-11 type call to her spouse in outcry about this supposed forcible rape. The fact that there were only two sentences of a synopsis in the law enforcement report tells me there was more to explain.

We began to attempt to interview this supposed outcry witness: the accuser's husband. He is a military officer and dodged my calls for weeks. I requested that my co-counsel make efforts, believing her military status might mean something to this officer. It did not. After ignoring our repeated phone calls and voicemails, we decided it was time to engage with his military superiors. He called my co-counsel back and screamed at her. Her colleague in the defense office wanted to intervene, but we preferred the spouse to let him do his worst; it would make better fodder for the eventual cross-examination we knew would come.

Finally, he submitted to a telephonic interview from my hotel room in Jackson, Wyoming on that rare day off from the Ranch. Four and a half hours later, we had learned a number of key facts. First, there had been no in the middle of the night outcry to the husband. He spoke to her the next morning on a regularly scheduled FaceTime call. You see, he was on temporary duty in Arizona. Second, the injuries he claimed to have seen were not anywhere close to the injuries she presented with several hours later at the hospital. We would learn that apparently she had used some kind of purple eye shadow to color her neck for their video chat. Third, the version of events that she gave to the husband was completely inconsistent with what she had told law enforcement.

That fish had gotten waaaaaay bigger. Fourth, we learned that whatever she described to him was not readily apparent criminal misconduct because his stated response to her was "well, I wasn't there so I cannot really tell you whether you should report or not." Because, wow, supportive husband.

Her spouse explained during this interview with us that he encouraged his wife to speak to her best gal pal to get her take on whether or not she should report. This would become incredibly important later. Fifth, we learned that the complainant's fourth husband – this witness was the fifth – was a man I served with in the Army and knew well. This was a huge investigative lead.

Our next interview was with the woman that the husband had told the accuser to contact to get advice about whether or not to report at all. I figured it would be rather nondescript – just a friend that told the accuser she should get medical treatment. What we found instead would mean the difference between a guilty verdict and proving the client's innocence.

The friend explained that the accuser had a sexual partner that had been "choking her" but the accuser became concerned when this man had left marks on her. This sexual partner was part of an on-going relationship and the markings from strangulation reportedly occurred weeks if not months before her one-night encounter with my client.

The friend encouraged the accuser to have a straightforward discussion with her partner, and the accuser, she said, seemed open to it. The accuser never called her friend to ask about reporting an assault. The accuser did speak with her friend about two weeks after she left the hospital the night that she did report.

In that discussion, the accuser told the friend that she had followed her prior advice to have a discussion with her on-going choking partner. The accuser told her gal friend that despite their talk, her partner had not listened; he got carried away and strangled her to the point where she passed out and when she came to, he had left the house. According to what the accuser told her friend, when she awakened, she got herself up and went immediately to the hospital where, according to the friend the accuser is diagnosed with a crushed windpipe. None of this happened and bore little resemblance to the report the accuser had given to law enforcement. She was identifying two separate men as the person who had strangled her.

Critically, the friend also shared with us that the accuser was part of a forced open marriage, that her husband expected her to hook up with strange men and then report back the details to him. If she declined, he said he would divorce her. This man was her fifth husband, and they share three children. That makes for a powerful reason to stage a rape: the threat of divorce if non-compliant with the open marriage, or to test his resolve.

Maybe, just maybe he would tell her she did not need to keep up her extra-marital relations. Maybe, she would be enough for him.

Military Rule of Evidence 412 permitted us to present evidence of an alternative source of injury: the prior mystery lover.

A closer look at the bruising showed that the injuries the accuser presented at the hospital were not acute, meaning they were older than 24 hours from the time they had been captured by the sexual assault nurse examiner.

There were after the fact text messages also that told two different aspects of the same tale. Approximately two weeks after their one and only sexual encounter, my client texted the accuser who had not yet filed any complaint He was inquiring about whether they could get together again. Her response? "Well, hello stranger." Because that's what you respond to a man who forcibly raped you by strangulation. Then "You call too late." Which necessarily invites an earlier call and a different result. After a few more text messages another night, he becomes frustrated and texts her "don't be that bitch." Within hours, the accuser goes to law enforcement to report a rape by strangulation.

Law enforcement encouraged her to perform pretext text messages to see if my client would make any admissions. He apologized in the messages for "getting carried away" and the government thought they had a slam-dunk given the physical injuries they were attributing to the client. They were wrong. And I had been wrong too. The government's mistake had been the same one that I had committed; they looked at the file and they looked no further. They did not dig, they did not examine, and they did not question.

I know that Daniel was meant to cross my path, and the phone call I made that hot July in 2018 confirmed it. The spouse of the complaining liar – I said what I said – made some oblique reference that made me realize that I knew the previous spouse of the alleged victim. Have you ever had an experience where seemingly unrelated tidbits of memories suddenly fire connections? Yeah. That.

The complainant's prior spouse and I had served together in the trenches of the Fort Hood Trial Defense Service. He was a jag and a fellow uniformed defense attorney. I recalled my buddy was going through a messy divorce.

He didn't seem inclined to talk about it, but of course, I made the offer to be a sympathetic ear if needed. Having gone through one or more divorces, I can also appreciate the strong inclination to keep your private life, private.

Believing that I knew the alleged victim's former spouse, I called and texted my friend, who had left the Army for greener pastures as a federal prosecutor. I mean, he's a real prosecutor: an assistant United States Attorney. I apologized to him for the need to call and explained that I hated to dig into his past, what might be painful memories. I'll never forget his reply: Your client is lucky to have you, and I wouldn't tell anyone else the things I am about to tell you.

This woman was a bona fide monster. She had made false allegations against my friend, which had been the subject of a previous investigation. Her lies were in print, were capable of being disproved, and her pattern for weaponizing allegations was ripe for my use. She had emotionally abused her own daughter, refusing to get her necessary medical and related behavioral health treatment. She made everything about her. Always. This was fitting the precise mold that I had sketched out when I began to dig into the case.

Effective trial representation is more than memorizing facts, dates, and times; it means appreciating the opponent, dissecting their psyche, and understanding that in emotions, motivation gels and takes form. What I came to know about this woman sickens me. Still, I had to go into the abyss to understand how anyone could set up a complete stranger to make it look like forcible rape. Teetering on that precipice between truth and understanding, there were moments I was not sure I would make it back. As in a handful of other cases, I tried to stave off the thoughts that if I somehow lost Daniel's case, I would not be able to get back into the arena. The weight of factual innocence is a crushing burden on the harbinger of truth.

More than a year after Daniel's full acquittal, he took his own life. He hanged himself in a lonely barracks room. I blame his accuser, I hold his idiot O-3 commander responsible, but if I am being 100% candid, I've taken on culpability myself because I couldn't save him. I didn't save him, not in the end. Not in the way that I knew that I could if only I would have reached out to him, or if he would have let me know of his pain.

As his mother comforted me after his passing, she thanked me for helping him through the darkest time of his life. I respectfully disagreed through streaming tears. Clearly, I had not.

Daniel and I shared the experience of leaving West Point shy of the goal of graduation. That is not easily describable to anyone who hasn't experienced it. I saw him as a kid brother that I wish that I had. There were times when he would not be reachable for communication, and I knew he was dipping dangerously into the dark place that my clients can easily visit, often to set up camp, and there are those who have not returned.

My team calls to them from across the shore, reminding them they are not alone, and that we can brace for the impact of battle together.

The most painful part of learning of Daniel's end was his mother sharing with me that he had a plan to surprise me one day at my office. He wanted to gather the wife he intended to marry and the children he planned to have with her and pop into my office one day. He longed to show me the life that my work allowed him to create for the world.

I won't get to meet those children, and I won't get to look at Daniel's smile or the way he closes his eyes and laughs effortlessly. No more laughs. No more jokes. His accuser took all of that from us. From the world.

I will never unburden myself fully from this pain; something like having eaten the fruit of the tree of knowledge. Once you've experienced such deep connection, the torment of its pain leaves an imprint, or better, scars. And not the gentle meandering ones. The jagged, Frankenstein's monster kind. Staples.

No matter the aching of the entire experience that remains for me and all who know that his accusations were impossible, I have to remind myself there is no greater honor than finding and keeping a friend for a lifetime.

Daniel's time on this earth was far too short, but I remain indebted to the time I was fortunate to spend in his company and in his inner circle.

When I represented the family at Daniel's military memorial at the on-post chapel, I had to curtly correct the Soldier who escorted me to my seat. I was not his lawyer; I was his friend.

I am grateful that Daniel showed immeasurable courage. He knew he was innocent. So, we went to work to prove it. And we did. But it came too late. And at too high a cost.

I pray others who know of the immeasurable grief that Daniel's last choice left on us will be moved to keep trudging through space and time. With honor.

Chapter 8

WAKE ME UP WHEN IT'S ALL OVER

A U.S. Soldier stationed in Germany finds himself in a nightmare from which he cannot awaken. Coming out of a fugue at the Provost Marshall's Office (PMO) in Vilseck, Germany with very few flash memories of the last twelve hours of his life, he is bloodied, bruised, his left knee swollen.

This particular Sunday morning, his nose is broken, he has a gash across his face, dried blood in his hair, and his knuckles and hands are swollen and bruised as though he has been in a fight, one he cannot recall.

A brief recollection of leaning up against a familiar club's bar taking a shot with a woman with long dark hair who's wearing a white shirt.

A snapshot of being struck in the side of the head with a metal object like a fry pan. A moment hiding behind a white trailer looking down at his hands, seeing blood and feeling hurt.

Grabbing a woman by the chin and demanding over and over to know what she did to him. Talking with an older woman, telling her that her husband is his father and feeling a sense of urgency to get to him. And blue flashing lights.

The familiar face of his NCO greets him at the Provost Marshall Office station and signs for his release. Sergeant P feels differently than he has ever felt. He is sluggish, even clouded, and normal tasks seem more difficult. He is not hungry, he feels nauseated, and different from any other hangover he has ever experienced. And he should know.

At that time in his life, Sergeant P was drinking often, to excess, and even had a tolerance so significant that he was able in one evening to finish two bottles of liquor. And still be functioning.

On this particular night, a witness reports that over the course of about six hours, he only drank between eight and ten drinks. For Sergeant P, the word only is appropriate.

My client tried the Army Substance Abuse Program once. But by his own self-report, his trusted counselor lost his job. Then they lost my client's records, and he got booted out of the system.

He knows this day he cannot account for what has happened, and he is scared for what he has done and afraid of what has happened to him. As he explains to his NCO what he knows from the night before, his fear grows.

After being dropped off, he eventually is able to shower, change clothes, and lays down to rest. Four hours later repeated knocks awaken him. It is his NCO again; it is time to go back to the PMO for his rights' warning. His first trip there, no one will advise him because a German breathalyzer at the scene of his arrest reported some amount of alcohol in his system. When advised of his legal rights, Sergeant P wisely invokes his right to counsel.

What he knows did not make sense to him at all, and he still isn't right.

He finally feels hung-over on Monday, though all of his symptoms do not fully subside until late Monday afternoon.

Monday evening, he sends a text message to his NCO informing him that he would like to take a drug test. Because he wants answers. After going through his chain of command, on Tuesday morning he is given the clear to submit samples.

He reports to the Grafenwoehr Troop Medical Clinic (TMC) and there, bureaucracy pushes back because of the length of time that has elapsed. Still, he insists on providing samples. The tech takes two blood vials and a urine sample.

The woman from the TMC calls him weeks later to report that his tests were negative. For what exactly, matters.

Before he hires me as his civilian counsel, his urine sample is destroyed. Yes, that's right.

And according to the government counsel, the blood vials were destroyed too. But then we found them. Sitting in a sub-contracting lab's storage in the United States.

And we, the defense, found the blood vials mere days before they were scheduled to be destroyed one year after receipt and one week before we were scheduled to go to trial the first time.

We submitted a request to the convening authority to fund private testing to run more than the standard drug screen panel that only tests for drugs like marijuana, cocaine, and run of the mill amphetamines. We were trying to search for the truth.

The convening authority denied our request. Shocker.

Faced with the risk of another continuance and dragging out this nightmare even longer by filing a motion to compel private funding, we opted not to. My client's family funded the private testing. They never stopped believing in him. They are parents who represent life goals for many of us.

After countless calls and Internet searches, I felt confident we found the best lab for private testing.

The first step was to establish that the blood sample really belonged to the client; with no evidentiary chain of custody, we wanted first to test a comparison DNA standard before we analyzed what substances were possibly remaining in his blood.

NMS Labs could perform both kinds of testing. And if the sample did not come back as consistent with our client's DNA, then we knew our search would cease.

Then, I was shocked when NMS Labs personnel explained we would never get a breakdown of all contents of the blood samples. Never stop learning, people.

NMS Labs personnel further explained that no lab provides a chemical analysis of every component of a given sample. Every lab possesses a library of component combinations to recognize a given drug, even synthetic drugs. If the given components in a submitted sample do not match one of their known standards from the library, NMS and other labs will not "call it." You'll never see peaks, charts, or data.

Despite the limitations of the science writ large, we chose NMS Labs because they have the largest library for comparison testing of all drugs to include synthetic and so called designer drugs. NMS Labs provides a list of tests from which you must choose, and each test carries its own separate fee. We wanted them all. We were searching for whatever had found its way into the Soldier's system.

A rush test with another fee, sample was confirmed to be the Soldier's by the statistic of 1 in 7 trillion. The known standard sample collected from the Soldier did not yield a full profile.

This means that the Military Police Investigator who took the sample from my client was inept at collecting a standard buccal swab. To not obtain a full profile from a known standard is pretty grave ineptitude because the sample is being tested from the inside of our client's mouth.

Whatever. We had his blood. We were encouraged and hopeful.

With only so many milliliters of blood, we had to prioritize our most likely candidates for analysis. After multiple tests, nothing was coming up and we were running out of the blood sample.

The government had turned over only one vial that the Soldier had provided and some of the sample had already been expended for the DNA test.

Now, you might be wondering or expecting that the government was conducting its own testing on the second blood vial, but fear not – no way.

The one fight in this war the government did not make us fight was releasing the second blood vial. Frankly, I believe someone figured out they had no grounds upon which to fight us – this was a privately given sample by the Soldier for medical treatment and not one based upon a probable cause seizure; and with their repeated singsong mantra that still echoes in my ears of "he was just drunk", I could hardly see them arguing to a military magistrate that probable cause existed to find evidence of a crime in his blood sample.

The government released the second vial to us. This meant that we had enough blood for all remaining tests.

So, we exhausted all avenues. Still the results were negative. For all drugs in the NMS Labs library collection. It was heartbreaking. But it was still a critical avenue for exploring.

There have been plenty of times in my career when I have made strategic decisions not to compel testing or not to explore certain investigative leads.

Many if not most or all of those decisions come after what I call a "come to Jocelyn" talk with the client. If I go down a certain avenue of investigation and it is visible or discoverable to the prosecution, I could harm my client.

In this case, I had no hesitation to explore all possible testing. I knew Sergeant P had been drugged without his knowledge, and that our theory of defense was reality.

Our forensic psychiatrist expert consultant reached out to a forensic toxicologist to help him understand about this library business and to help us understand how best potentially to explain the absence of any positive test results.

The first explanation was easiest to understand – there had been a significant time lapse between ingestion and sample collection, which made it difficult but not impossible to find the substance. The second explanation was unexpected – the duration that the sample went untested made the predictability of detection virtually unpredictable.

No one knows or understands how synthetic compounds, like bath salts, are preserved in bodily fluids after storage for a long period of time. The third related explanation dealt with unknown variables in the manner the sample was stored, and we knew very little about how the sample had been stored for that time over one year.

We strategized whether to turn it all over to the government, and my inclination was to. The results, the explanation, everything. Even though the government was aware of the fact that we were conducting testing, there remained an argument that they were not entitled to know the results of private defense efforts.

My thinking was that despite the negative results, we needed to be open and explain to the panel *why* we had no positive test results. Note: the defense has no affirmative obligation to turn over any information which is not favorable to the accused or any materials the defense has in its possession that we do not intend to introduce or upon which no witness has based their testimony or opinion.

But... if I wanted to point out the lackluster investigation the government conducted, there might be a way for a prosecutor to let the panel know we had pursued testing but weren't revealing the results. Trials are competitions for credibility. Defense attorneys clamor for every morsel of it from jury panels, and it will disintegrate from the courtroom if they learn you're hiding something.

Our expert explained the negative test results did not change his opinion that the Soldier's *behavior* was consistent with a drug induced delirium and that in the state of delirium he would not have been able to appreciate the nature, quality, and wrongfulness of his actions. His inability to recall events prior to any ingestion at the club known as retrograde amnesia was a telltale sign of a drugging.

So, we handed over everything. The DNA report, the negative test results, articles upon which the expert was relying to explain the absence of the positive result, and information on drug induced delirium. We declared our expert consultant as a witness, and we waited for the government to arrange an interview in advance of trial. But the government prosecutors did not call our expert.

Days later, in fact, the day before our last day of preparation, the government filed a motion to preclude the expert's testimony, which meant a motion to preclude essentially our entire defense. The basis? Lack of notice. And a *Daubert* challenge. That's lawyer-speak for them alleging our expert's opinion was not sufficiently based in reliable science. Because we had no positive drug test, and according to them, "he was just drunk." Oh, and also, our expert was only a forensic toxicologist. But guess what? Our expert witness is a forensic psychiatrist.

Did the Government bother to read any of the science in this field or even read the notice of expert testimony we provided? It would appear not so.

Defense requested to litigate the government motion first thing the day of trial and to delay the trial by an hour, but the government insisted we litigate the motion during a time they knew we had plans to interview all of the local national witnesses. Because, you know, justice.

Defending a case while positioned geographically in another country, there are challenges based solely on time zone. Add language barriers and the need for translators to the mix, and you have a downright gnarly knot.

I filed our motion response at 1:51am local time. The one to challenge the government's effort to preclude our entire defense.

I finished the rest of my prep save witness interviews around 4am.

Part of my response to the government's motion documented that the government counsel had not bothered to interview our expert, so it was difficult for me to understand a *Daubert* challenge without a report or summary of expected testimony of a prosecution expert.

The government sent an email relaying that if the judge did not grant their motion to preclude the expert testimony, they would seek continuance due to the late notice of our defense of involuntary intoxication, which according to their pleading had not been given until the 21st of January 2017.

In order to defend against this insinuation of late notice, my motion response included documentation that six months before the government obtained an expert consultant in the same field, and their justification was that the defense was using the defense of... wait for it, involuntary intoxication.

Our original formal notice of special defenses had been disclosed on the 8th of August 2016 that the defense intended to "likely use the defense of innocent ingestion." After the filing of the defense motion response, the government deigned to finally interview our expert witness. I thought for a brief moment the government might withdraw its motion, at least on *Daubert* grounds since the attorney must surely have realized the reliability and how the testimony would be helpful to the trier of fact. But, gosh, that never came either.

After several hours on the record laying out the expert's testimony, its reliability, and basis, the military judge ruled against the government's challenge to preclude his testimony. I have a hard time imagining that anyone in that room believed the judge would ever grant the government's motion, but it was filed to waste our time in preparation. Bravo, government! And to try to justify continuance. Those are your tax dollars hard at work.

In the judge's chambers, the government counsel had the audacity to propose continued trial dates which they had "taken the liberty" of clearing with the judge's calendar and their own. But not mine.

After explaining that I was not available for this date almost a month out, defense opposed continuance beyond an hour to give the government time to consult with their own expert in the same field.

And then, during litigation, when I formally opposed the government's request for continuance, the proverbial cat came screeching out of the bag… the government had not travelled their expert to trial. The government explained that they needed the time to secure a rebuttal witness because the defense expert would not admit on cross-examination that all of the Soldier's signs and symptoms could be explained by him "just being drunk." See retrograde amnesia.

I opposed the judge's consideration of any delay based merely on the proffer of government counsel. I could not envision the government finding any witness to testify that the Soldier's signs and symptoms were consistent with alcohol intoxication alone. Because science.

The only hang up was that defense still had not yet received the affidavit from a forensic toxicologist that explained the issues with storage and time lapse in sample testing. The government's point was that they could not fairly meet our expert without having all of the data upon which he was basing his testimony. That's a fair point.

Thankfully, the military judge denied the government's continuance but warned us that if defense had not disclosed the affidavit by morning, he would revisit the government's motion for continuance. We turned over the affidavit at 9:52pm local time as soon as we received it from the toxicologist. Remember time zone challenges? Yeah, those.

Despite the government's attempts to gain tactical advantage and to derail our preparation, we laid out concrete evidence that the Soldier was drugged. Even without a positive drug test. Then came the government's Hail Mary...

On cross-examination of our expert witness, the government suggested that my client knowingly ingested whatever drug caused his psychotic behavior. The only way that an involuntary intoxication defense works is if this Soldier ingested the substance unwittingly, so by suggesting he ingested the drug on purpose, they were going with an insulting "plan B."

I'm not sure why I was so surprised; it was more of the same. In hindsight a better capture of my feeling was more disgust than anything. The Soldier's service record was pristine, and the government could not find one infraction in his past or any misbehavior since his arrest more than a year before his trial.

I railed away on the government for their inept investigation by failing to collect blood and urine right away, you know, after the guy is delusional and screaming at an 82 year-old German woman that her husband is his father. Likewise, I thundered away at them for the government's eleventh hour baseless assertion that involuntary intoxication should not defend the Soldier's actions because he must have knowingly taken drugs. They argued he took these unknown drugs to "build his confidence to talk to a girl at a bar and dance with her" and to "celebrate his approved Medical Evaluation Board." It made no sense. Not their evolving theory, and not their conduct as the supposed guardians of truth. Their sense of justice needs some reimaging.

The panel saw the evidence for what it was: clear and convincing evidence of involuntary intoxication, a complete defense to all charged misconduct.

And the panel reached their conclusion in only 24 minutes. They saw what the government had been ignoring for months. Because as I hissed during my closing argument, the government attorneys "care more about winning, than they do about justice."

Sergeant P's nightmare was finally over.

We will never know what chemicals made their way into his system, or even concretely who is to blame for drugging him.

There are hours of his life unaccounted for, and those responsible for beating him will go unpunished. What precisely were their motives or how many people were working in concert will not be revealed.

But in the verdict's, the risk of conviction, jail time, and a punitive discharge had evaporated. A good man was set free.

My hope is that training is implemented to teach responders to recognize the symptoms of surreptitious drugging. There need to be processes to detect these compounds. Blood and urine samples should be taken in any instance that looks like a "DUI pickup" where the symptoms are not consistent with only alcohol. Hint: delusions. Synthetic drugs are dangerous, and U.S. service members, particularly those serving abroad, are vulnerable to being targeted.

Tragedy abounds: this fine Soldier was forced to live a nightmare for fifteen months. Also, there is too great a potential for future tragedy in all of this – those who work in this prosecutor's office came away from this trial believing that a slick lawyer helped thwart justice. I'm not sure if they would recognize justice if it hit them in the side of their head with a fry pan.

What remains after the fugue are the Christmas cards from the client's family that lovingly litter my desk in downtown Tacoma. I won't throw away any of them.

As the years melt away, I half expect that I have seen the last. So far, they haven't. They include updates of his success and remain a corporal reminder of the pride I feel in getting to stand up for him.

Jocelyn C. Stewart

Chapter 9

FLYING FOR CARPETS

Sometimes justice requires a field trip.

In this case, it required me to go to Iraq. Before I could go to Iraq, though, I had to go through Soldier Readiness Processing (SRP). At Fort Hood, Texas.

On November 4, 2009, I completed dental readiness. I called the Officer in Charge (OIC) of the SRP site and explained that I needed to deploy to Iraq as an Individual Augmentee (IA). He explained that a reserve unit would be going through the next day and that I should try to arrive between 10:00am and 10:30am.

I recall sitting at my desk when the reminder dinged on my government computer, prompting me to head to the SRP site. On November 5th, 2009.

I considered all of the other obligations that I had to balance, and I decided I wasn't going. The government and their stupid deposition would have to wait.

This is the one and only time that I have blown off a work obligation. Ever.

At approximately 1:30pm on November 5th, 2009, Major Nidal Hasan entered the SRP site at Fort Hood and opened fire. He killed thirteen people and injured more than thirty others. And I was supposed to be there. But I wasn't.

In an earlier chapter, I explained how I was left in charge of the Fort Hood Trial Defense Service Office that week because our senior defense counsel and regional defense counsel were in D.C. for the leadership conference.

Initially, news media outlets were reporting that there were three live shooters acting in concert. My instruction from leadership was that I would be detailed to the first shooter who invoked his right to counsel. I would then be tasked with assigning attorneys to represent the other two shooters. "Who?" I asked. No one else in our region had experience in homicide cases, and my then spouse was another of the uniformed attorneys in our defense office. It would be an ethical conflict for my spouse to be assigned one of the shooters if I was already handling another shooter's case.

Then, news broke that there was only one shooter, and preliminary reports at that time indicated that he was dead. I was relieved. We all were. Until we weren't. Hours later we learned Major Hasan was still alive.

My boss, the senior defense counsel, returned from D.C. and let me know that when Major Hasan finally asked for counsel or whenever he was formally charged, I would be his lawyer.

Thirty minutes later, my boss walked back into my office; his already pale skin was wallpaper paste grey. Higher headquarters had intervened and decried that "Jocelyn isn't to touch this case." They didn't want to "ruin" my career.

Can we just take a pause for a moment and consider the idea that *defending* a high profile murder case was being seen through the lens of ruining a career? What?! I had already been identified as the Midwest's Special Victim Prosecutor, so I was already supposed to be on my way out of the door. Perhaps that's what they meant...

At that time, my boss was tasked with leading the military's busiest court-martial jurisdiction in the world. But he had never defended a Soldier in his life. Yep, that's right.

Please do not think these personnel selections occur by accident. Priorities are not given to defense offices. Not then, and not now.

Our higher headquarters sent word that my boss would be Major Hasan's trial attorney. At least as a placeholder. A dear friend and respected colleague, (then) Lieutenant Colonel Kris Poppe would be detailed four or five weeks later. Thank heaven. I could not wait to stop watching the trainwreck that was unfolding around me. Major Hasan's initial civilian defense counsel spent his time tweeting instead of preparing, and my boss was running to my office periodically to try to share with me the horrors he was learning on the case. Calgon, take me away.

That SRP site had become a crime scene. I would go through SRP months later at another location so I could take that field trip to Iraq. Aside over.

My E-7 client had been accused of stealing carpets from a carpet salesperson who was operating on the base in Iraq via Morale Welfare Recreation, what we call MWR for short. He was also charged with stealing a credit card from a fellow service member on deployment.

In reviewing his charge sheet and the accompanying investigation packet, I see a summary of a verbal statement that was given to law enforcement by the Turkish bazaar carpet salesman. He explains that he sold some carpets to my client, and later it turned out that the client had supposedly used a stolen credit card to pay for the carpets.

The investigation packet contained a customs declaration indicating the client had mailed carpets back to the U.S. from the base in Iraq and that they had been intercepted in the U.S. by law enforcement. Army CID documented the seizure with photographs of the carpets. Sigh.

Things weren't looking good for the "home team." He was looking mighty guilty.

Almost every investigation packet I review makes the accused look solidly guilty. Military law enforcement doesn't exactly do a bang up job of looking at alternative theories.

Best news in the file? This E-7 had not given a statement to the cops. Invocation much? Yes, please. At least we had that going for us. And yes, though it is a process that is occurring to him, there is an us. Every defense counsel and client are a team.

I was anxious to hear the client's explanation to account for the evidence that was being levied against him.

That discussion changed everything.

One of the glaring absences in the file that I had not even realized was an issue until we spoke, was that there was no inventory by the carpet store to reflect that these, or any carpets, were the property of the Turkish carpet store.

Why would that matter? Because these carpets actually belonged to my E-7 client.

Setting out to prove ownership of the carpets would be the singular goal of our defense.

Recall that documentation where my client's customs declaration announced he was shipping carpets back to the U.S.? This was two-edged. Notably, there's a lot of really dumb criminals in the world. Let's just get that out there in the open. Even still, I am trying to consider my client's story to me that these "stolen" carpets were in fact his own, it had seemed really strange to me that if he stole carpets, that he's going to admit that's what he was shipping on his customs form.

For anyone who has deployed, it does not seem

altogether unusual to ship personal items back to yourself at the end of the tour.

One of the other things that also stood out to me in this packet was the way that this alleged larceny had come to light.

The credit card holder was a Chief Warrant Officer from a different but neighboring military organization. He was reviewing his credit card statement online and saw that there were some substantial charges to a credit card that he had not used while he was deployed.

Dutifully, the Chief Warrant Officer reported the fraudulent charges to his credit card, but he didn't stop there. He did some of the investigation's leg work. The Warrant Officer spoke to a representative from the MWR facility because what had been reflected on the charge was a charge from MWR, but not which vendor had charged it. The MWR representative traced the charge to the Turkish carpet vendor at the bizarre. When the MWR employee spoke to the Turkish carpet salesman, the salesman said that he had sold carpets for that transaction to my client, the E-7.

Note: He got set up.

Why would the carpet salesman lie? Why would he point to my client as the culprit? And how would he even know that my client had carpets in his possession?

The client explained that he actually knew this carpet salesman. Say what? Okay. How do you know him? My E-7 client starts explaining to me that over the course of his many, many years in service and his many, many deployments, he had become very interested in and knowledgeable about Turkish carpets. He is a collector.

Through his deployments and hobby of buying carpets, he had educated himself about the different kinds of carpets and all the different kinds of materials that they're made with, even the mechanisms of how they're made. By viewing the backing of the carpet, he can tell whether it has been made by hand versus a machine.

As a result of his hobby, he approached and befriended the Turkish carpet salesman who is now identifying him as the culprit in some theft. He develops rapport with the MWR carpet salesman by talking about his collection over tea.

My client was describing his collection to the salesman.

According to the E-7, several of his carpets are quite valuable.

During their discussions, the carpet salesman says to my client that he believes my client has been duped, that he could not possibly possess the quality of carpets he believes that he paid for. The salesman offers to inspect the carpets to give him an honest appraisal.

My client goes home during his mid tour leave from deployment, retrieves several of the carpets, and travels back to Iraq with them. The E-7 explains to me that the carpets he was shipping back to the U.S. were part of his personal collection that he was sending back home.

As a rule, I never blindly accept the story a client gives me. I wouldn't be doing my job if I did.

I start checking out the E-7 client's story to ascertain if he had a collection of carpets.

It is not as simple as retrieving banking records or credit card statements because most of these transactions are occurring off installation at a local bizarre.

For cash.

We found 25 witnesses who were able to attest to my client's history of collecting Turkish carpets and to his knowledge of carpets.

I nearly fell out of my chair when my client explained that his roommate may have seen him come home during his mid-tour leave to package up some of these carpets to take back to Iraq with him. The roommate did corroborate that the client owned several carpets, that he kept many of them in a certain location in the house. He explained that the client owned so many of them that many were not in use.

Those that were being stored were rolled up and wrapped in thick, protective plastic. The roommate recalled my client packing up something to take back with him back to Iraq, though he wasn't exactly sure what that was.

As a former prosecutor and skeptical defense attorney, it crossed my mind that these friends could be fabricating their potential testimony to help protect their friend.

There was still the issue of the credit card theft from the Chief Warrant Officer and the credit card transaction from the installation MWR vendor.

According to the Warrant Officer, he kept his credit card in his locked containerized housing unit (CHU). How would my client possibly have gained access to a locked CHU from a different organization across the base? I checked on potential access through master keys maintained by members of the respective unit. Nada.

And then I started to put it together.

What helped me to understand the many permutations of why and how the Turkish carpet salesman would fabricate a story against the E-7 client was the in-person investigation that I conducted while in Iraq. Typically, the government will not fund travel for defense investigation unless the case involves a deployed shooting. In this case, the government needed the trip for their prosecution.

The government had realized that they could not produce their star witness for trial because the State Department had denied them a VISA. They said this salesman was too great a risk for remaining illegally in the U.S. after the need for his presence concluded. Enter the need for a trip to Iraq to depose the Turkish national.

A deposition is a tool that is used often in civil lawsuits but are exceedingly rare in military court-martial practice. In two decades, I have been a part of three depositions, and I believe that is two more than anyone else that I have practiced   with   or   against.

Other than the individuals living in each CHU, the only people with access to the living quarters were people who were contracted to clean them. What I surmised but could not prove was that this carpet salesman was fencing stolen credit cards through the business and partnering with the cleaning contractor who obtained access to credit cards that service members were rarely using and rarely checking on. Under this scheme, the contractor would slip the stolen credit cards to someone with a credit card machine, get a cut. Lather, rinse, repeat.

How many people on deployment are keeping track of charges on credit cards that they aren't using? The fact that this charge was discovered as quickly as it was felt rare and only thanks to the Chief Warrant Officer's vigilance.

Key to the ability to run this fence was that MWR had no way of even verifying that any merchandise was exchanged for any given credit card transaction. There were no inventories to prove that one day a given carpet was in the possession of the vendor and the next week's inventory showed they had one less. The only record was a chart that was filled out by hand to annotate the charge –

that was all MWR requested from a given vendor. In seeing this massive vacancy of records, I had to appreciate on some level that this was a pretty smart operation.

In addition to my desire to be face to face in speaking with the MWR manager to understand their records system, or really a lack of one, I wanted to speak with people about the key access issue. There was also this pesky matter of the government's deposition of the carpet salesman.

The government was attempting to preserve his testimony for use at my client's trial.

In criminal cases in the military, caselaw has made it exceedingly difficult to introduce depositions in lieu of live testimony. And with good reason. The crucible of cross-examination is the purest way to seek the truth, and a jury should be able to watch and decipher credibility from watching the person squirm or not as the witness is made to answer tough and pointed questions.

The easiest way to keep out a deposition from evidence in trial is to demonstrate that at the time of the questioning the defense did not have a key piece of information about which they were unable to cross-examine the witness during the deposition. Always seek more discovery. Particularly after a deposition.

As taxpayers, each of you should feel genuine concern over the fact that the expense of traveling a prosecutor, court reporter, the defense attorneys, and the client cost more in airfare alone than was the alleged loss in value of the carpets they believed my client had stolen. Yeah.

Back to how the salesman decided to choose the E-7 as his patsy.

When my client had returned to Iraq with the carpets, he presented them to the salesman who promised to advise him about whether his carpets were in reality of the caliber that he believes. You're going to be shocked, but the salesman says words to the effect that precisely as he had suspected, the client has been ripped off. The salesman alleges that the carpets are machine made and very cheap. He doesn't stop there. He says as a friend, he wants to help my client, that he will take the carpets off his hands. My client politely declines this generous offer. Uh huh.

So, this carpet salesman knows that my client is in possession of Turkish carpets. An easy fall guy when the stolen credit card transaction is discovered.

Oh, by the way, the carpets were legit. We had them appraised. Enter secondary and convenient motivation to fabricate allegations that my client had stolen these particular carpets from them. While the investigation as taking place, the salesman kept asking when the carpets would be returned to *his* possession. He wanted them badly.

While in Iraq, I become extremely ill. Can we say burn pits? Burn pits.

I completely lost my voice. There's mucus abounding, and I am a snotty disgusting mess. Jet lagged and miserable. Given the dust, the poor air quality, and these burn pits that are adjacent to the CHU where I am being housed, I become undeniably sick. An attorney without a voice is like a morning without a sunrise. Or whatever.

After some good old fashioned medical malpractice thanks to an E-4 at the 1st Cavalry Division's clinic after voice rest and 800 mg Motrin® failed, I somehow manage to get some semblance of my voice back.

The government prosecutor goes first in his questioning of the salesman at the deposition because this salesman is his witness. Everything is progressing, no issues. The Turkish carpet salesman's English is fine. He's communicating, he's understanding their questions, even though some of them are compound and not the best phrased. He's doing fine.

Wouldn't you know, as soon as I switch over to cross examination, suddenly, the salesman insists he cannot understand my questions. He claims his English is suddenly poor. He will not proceed, contending he requires a translator. Okay buddy. We'll play that game. For a little while.

After a break and some minor bullying, the deposition continues.

Preliminaries aside, I get to the heart of the inquisition. I look him in the eye, and I ask him "where did those carpets come from?" He pauses and then he responds, "Turkey." He thinks he's cute. He's not. The carpets clearly came from Turkey, but he knows what I'm asking. He knows. I replied thank you for that. They come from Turkey. Where did they specifically come from?

After a significant pause, the salesman sticks to his story, and he says they were his. I take him through the fact that there's no inventory, there's no proof that these carpets were ever in his possession. I mess with him a little bit, and I highlight that he has never talked to my client's roommate. He has no knowledge about witnesses who saw my client purchase each carpet, retrieve the carpets, and travel back to Iraq with them. He sticks to his story, but he's all over the place.

We wrap up the deposition. I'm a little bit worse for the wear given my barely recovered voice after temporary laryngitis. We travel back together and are relieved that we avoided being extended in Iraq. Sandstorm season is approaching. In the ramp up to trial, our witness list is substantial.

We had also amassed a hefty patchwork of records from the time periods of the purchases of these carpets. Bank records reflect cash withdrawals correlating to the right timeframes and carpet prices.

Friends of my client had varying degrees of what each could recall. Everyone seemed to recall a pink carpet in particular because they had teased my client for buying a shade so "feminine."

I am certain that was not the verbiage they used.

I would have been suspicious if each witness would have recalled in vivid detail the specifics of each carpet. Their recollections seemed to be what I would expect given the time that had passed and what would make sense for them to recall. Each of them had their piece of the puzzle and nobody's memory was perfect, but it seemed plausible. We also stacked our witness list with a nearly ridiculous number of good military character witnesses.

Congress has taken away a military accused's right to defend specific allegations with good military character evidence. Sexual assault chief among them. Character defense persists though for a good number of allegations. Larceny remains one.

Our plan at trial also included calling witnesses to attest to the E-7's character for truthfulness, which becomes relevant if the client testifies in his own defense.

No matter how confident I can feel about any given case, at their core, jury trials are human processes. And humans err. Given this truth and the pressures and stress that trials place on the accused client, my preference and my goal in every case is to kill it before we ever get to trial. My ego doesn't need to hear the words "not guilty." Dismissal is always preferred.

After amassing our substantial list of witnesses and marking a hefty number of exhibits, the government finally caved. Three days prior to trial the government dismissed all charges. "In the interests of justice." It would take several years for this client to earn his deserved promotion to E-8 and all of the backpay it warranted.

Dismissal was the right result, but this allegation should not have resulted in the months long ordeal and a costly, dangerous trip to Iraq. The presumption of innocence should mean something.

In Iraq, my client was not allowed to carry a weapon. Anyone who has ever deployed knows that you cannot eat in a dining facility without a weapon. Not only did they send him to a war zone to defend himself against spurious allegations, but they also wouldn't permit him the entitlement of protecting himself or of even having an easy way to eat. I had to eat in advance of him and then hand him my weapon so then he could go eat. Disgraceful conduct by thoughtless government actors.

The guardians of justice must do better.

Master Sergeant, it has been my honor.

Chapter 10

INSTAGRAM® INSANITY

Whoever thought that a one specification drug case would require twenty-one witnesses to prove innocence? No one who was watching the insanity from the sideline, that's who. But that's precisely what happened in Courtroom 2 at the Cascade Courtroom Complex in December of 2022.

After this grueling battle, it took a while for me to really recover from fatigue and stress, even not being able to eat or sleep much during this trial. This one definitely felt personal.

Major Joann LeDoux was charged with having tested positive for amphetamines from a urinalysis that she gave as part of her organization's 100% collection. She is a medical provider who has knowledge certainly of amphetamines generally. So, when she tested positive, she received notification in late September of 2021.

She contacted me almost right away, and we had a consultation in early October.

Whenever someone is looking to me for a potential representation on a positive urinalysis case, I always ask whether the person is willing to submit another urine sample for private testing. And a hair follicle test.

Hair follicle tests are not infallible, but they are generally good at detecting whether there has been long-term use as opposed to a one-time use.

So, despite the limitation of hair follicle testing, I ask would-be clients to submit for it as a good faith showing on their part that they really don't know where the detected substance came from. It's also a small financial buy-in. I do a fair number of consultations with people who claim that they didn't knowingly use and when asked if they'll pay for and provide these tests for my eyes only, that seems to weed out a lot of people. No pun intended. Joann gladly said she would, and she did.

In addition to the long-term versus one-time usage limitation in hair follicle testing, there was also an issue of what kinds of amphetamines the commercially available test could detect. The results simply said negative for amphetamines, although the report didn't exactly give us the exculpatory evidence we originally thought.

The online representations of the testing facility led any reasonable person to believe that the test would give us information about all classes of amphetamines, including d-amphetamines, l-amphetamines, and methamphetamines. But they could not.

When Major LeDoux went online to request the urine and hair follicle tests, the lab's explanation was that it would perform a five panel urine screen and a five panel hair follicle test. Specifically, the test indicated it would look for "amphetamines (including methamphetamine and MDEA and MEA)." So, both of us felt good about choosing the screen.

While we were awaiting the results, we worked together to author a full statement to military law enforcement. We wanted to pass along our suspicion that the reason she had tested positive in this case was from contaminated or adulterated supplements that she had been taking. It's a really scary thing. This was my first case that really dived very deeply into supplements and the world that is supplements that is so very unregulated and potentially dangerous.

Army Major Joann LeDoux, like many, was questioning a lot about her life. She felt drawn to make positive change. She wanted to get fit, reclaim her power: mind, body, and spirit. Online promises of clarity, concentration, focus, and motivation sounded like precisely what she wanted. The advertising was dialed in, for sure.

In examining this issue regarding the sales of supplements I discovered its lack of regulation. Wherever you sit on the scale of wanting big or small government, when contaminated supplements find their way to consumers, everyone loses.

When Joann received the phone call from her commander notifying her of the positive result, she was about to head into a yoga class. She paused, took the call, and her life would never be the same. He explained that her routine urinalysis had come back positive for amphetamines.

What?! How?

This commander would later testify in her felony level court-martial that she was in utter shock and disbelief at the news.

The call ended rather quickly, and Joann decided the best thing for her to do in that moment was to try to block out all of the worry and anxiety this call delivered to her, to try to be present during her yoga practice. She managed to, and then retreated to her car right after class sobbing. Lost and unsure.

She started to drive home, only to need to pull over. She could not see the road through her cascading tears. Joann called a close friend, another Army officer, also a nurse. As she sat there in her car, they ran over all possible scenarios. What had changed between all of her other routine urine samples and this latest one?

There was only one possible explanation: the nootropics supplements she had purchased through an ad on Instagram®.

As we talked about the case during that critical investigative stage, I learned that she still had some of the supplements, although they were not from the first box of the "subscription" she had paid for. This would prove extremely important later.

We got the tests results back from the urine and hair samples Major LeDoux had provided for private testing. Both results stated that they were negative for all five classes of drugs including amphetamines. We're feeling like maybe we can stop this train before it's coming full steam at her and over her.

I assisted Joann in writing that statement to law enforcement. Through counsel. Always through counsel. We provided substantial details about the company, her purchases, the timeline, what representations were made about these supplements, and our fear that they must be the source for the positive urinalysis. We even explained to the investigator that we welcomed them collecting the remaining supplements to test for contamination.

You're going to be utterly shocked that the government did not follow up to collect the supplements from Major LeDoux. No really.

What we were trying to stop, among other processes, was the titling and indexing that occurs when a member of law enforcement decides there was probable cause to believe a crime was committed. This lasts in a person's record for forty years. Yep.

Despite my best efforts, the very junior prosecutor supported the Army investigator's position that probable cause existed. And he didn't stop there. This prosecutor authored an email that stated there were no other reasonable investigative leads to pursue in the case.

Um, hello – supplement testing much?

That email would later land him a place on the defense witness list.

Included in the statement we gave to law enforcement was the specific company that sold them to her, the listed ingredients of the supplements, all of the research she did before taking them, and photographs of the supplements that she still had in her possession. After she stopped taking them, one more monthly subscription had arrived.

On Instagram®, Joann had filled out an online quiz that was supposed to hone in on what it was that she was looking for within the classification of supplements called nootropics. The company was peddling this idea that their product is good for brain health. They asserted in advertising that they had amassed substances that can provide clarity, motivation, focus, and energy. You should be seeing where this is going.

We also highlighted in her statement to the authorities that Joann had provided a number of vials of blood as part of a volunteer study to look into the long-term effects of medical providers who had to work through COVID-19. At the time we provided this information to law enforcement we didn't know if the blood was still available for testing or even if the data gleaned from the testing that had already occurred was within the control of the military.

Additionally, we provided a copy of the private urine sample testing results to show that at least as of the time of giving that sample, she no longer had amphetamines in her system. As soon as she was made aware that she had tested positive, she had discontinued any use of these supplements. We were trying to show the correlation between her ceasing the ingestion of the supplements and the subsequent negative result.

So, looking at all the data that we had, our respectful ask was to please come collect the supplements. Please come test them. Please go look for her blood. Please do an actual investigation.

We also kindly offered that if there were any follow on questions that they had for her to please, please provide them so that we could review and answer. I was open to the idea that there was information I had overlooked that might prove helpful in demonstrating Joann's factual innocence.

When law enforcement refused, I know that I should not have been surprised, or hurt, or angry. The "investigator" on the case had been a Military Policeman for a couple of years and was designated to work over at what's called the Drug Suppression Team (DST). This team works as part of the Army's Criminal Investigative Division. And most of the military law enforcement agencies have their own version of the DST. They are charged with "investigating" every positive urinalysis case, which mostly means they work to obtain confessions. They're also tasked with investigating cases where service members introduce drugs onto the installation, and at times, coordinating undercover buys to find those in the food chain of drug distribution.

The rather inexperienced investigator presented the materials we provided to his supervisor.

According to both of their testimony, the supervisor told the investigator no investigative leads regarding the supplements needed to be explored. Oh joy, your tax dollars hard at work trying to "seek the truth."

The military justice advisor echoed that he saw no need to investigate any further. Later when questioned on the stand during the trial, he swore under oath that he ran this opinion past his Chief of Military Justice, who is the senior prosecutor. According to him, the Chief of Military Justice also said no further action was needed. And they took no further steps.

They did nothing. They didn't talk to anyone at the unit to see if they'd seen any behavioral changes in Joann. They took no investigative steps to see if she ever had or would've had access to the amphetamines in question.

Understand that Major LeDoux was and remains a medical provider, but she is someone who performs anesthesia as a nurse. This means she has access to sedatives, things that knock you out, things that make you unconscious so that you can go through surgery. Not uppers like amphetamines.

In approaching the case, I knew that I would need the help of multiple experts. Typically, these experts are funded by the government. Yes, you read that right. As long as I can justify expertise is necessary to a fair trial, the prosecution picks up the tab.

There is a substantial difference in the standards for obtaining an expert consultant versus an expert witness. When asking for a forensic consultant who will also be enveloped in the attorney client privilege, you must be mindful that if I ask for a very expensive private one, the government actors typically turn those down. That necessitates added time and energy to litigate a motion to compel in front of the military judge. You also must be mindful that the standard is quite high to have a judge compel an expert consultant. So, whenever possible, I look within the Department of Defense and find experts who are free other than the cost of their travel and per diem because they are government employees.

In this case, I reached out and found a forensic toxicologist who was working out of the Fort Sam Houston / San Antonio area. He was approved, but the government turned down our forensic chemist *witness* from NSF International.

NSF International is an accrediting certifying body for various labs and various manufacturers and producers of, among other things, supplements. They also have purview over substances that are banned among elite athletes. In short, they set protocols for what's banned in sports and give guidance and oversight.

Through some contacts, I reached out and found someone from NSF International who was actually willing to aid us at no additional cost for consultation and testimony. It had been an NSF International laboratory who had performed the testing of the supplements Major LeDoux still had in her possession. We had been looking for direct evidence of adulteration with amphetamines in the supplements that she still had control over. It would be very significant in the case that we did not have the actual supplements from the initial batch that she had been taking at the time she tested positive.

One of the things that I came to learn in this supplement industry is that they will, if they're unsavory, they may adulterate their product with something addictive early on in the subscription and then rely on the placebo effect after that. It is certainly expensive to put Adderall® and other similar amphetamines into a commercial supplement to make people want to keep taking them. They can't do it forever, but if they are doing it intentionally, they do it early.

Because of this practice, we were certainly open to a new working hypothesis that we may not actually find anything in the supplements we still had. I still felt like we needed to try. When you are presenting a case that your client is factually innocent, each step in independent defense investigation takes on three roles: 1) looking for actual exculpatory evidence; 2) demonstrating that you, the defense, are seeking the truth, even if it does not lead to bear fruit; and 3) the client's behavior that would be inconsistent with her having knowingly ingested unlawful substances.

When NSF International detected no amphetamines, it was certainly frustrating. Recall that we didn't have the specific batch of supplements that she was taking at the time of her urinalysis. She had consumed all of that initial monthly subscription because of the delay in testing of her urine sample and in it being reported to her chain of command and her subsequent notification. But we were willing to try. The client paid quite a bit of money for private testing at NSF International.

I don't know that I've thought more about pending results in my life. I was hoping that we could catch a break and that the testing would show definitively that these supplements were the source of Joann's amphetamine positive. I was almost willing it to be so. In consulting with the expert from NSF International, he informed me he felt like it was a strong possibility given some of what had been reflected on the corporation's advertising. He noted some red flags from their website also.

My desperate hope was that the results would end in dismissal. Much earlier in my career, I adopted the philosophy that winning a trial without needing to have a trial was the ultimate victory. As I sat at the counsel table with my clients, I did not see cases, I saw people. Humans who were being put through the trauma of false accusations; it takes its toll on them and even on the litigators. Vicarious trauma and all.

When discussing the results with the expert from NSF International, he informed me that not even all of the substances that they alleged were in their product were actually included.

I was more than disappointed; I was saddened. I had to remind myself that our broader strategy in this case was to let the panel see that all of these actions that she was taking after learning about her positive urinalysis were not the actions of a person who had knowingly used an illicit substance. We call this circumstantial evidence of the absence of knowledge or intent. The idea is that if Major LeDoux knows that she was ingesting this substance, why would she risk so much? Why would she pay so much in private testing? Why would she keep trying to find the truth? Even though the testing could not detect amphetamines in the supplements, the fact that we had contracted for private testing was a fact we wanted to introduce at trial.

As we geared up for the first trial dates, which were in August of 2022, I became increasingly frustrated that the government had not made positive contact with the person at the lab who would be able to lay the foundation for the results of Major LeDoux's private hair follicle and urine sample testing. In fact, it ended up causing a several month continuance, which is why we did not try the case until mid-December 2022.

At the trial, we also offered into evidence the contents of Joann's cell phone. This data included biometrical data of her vital signs, sleep patterns, calls, texts, GPS location movements, and even her shopping and banking habits. Initially, we pursued this investigative lead privately through a digital media company who I use almost exclusively for my cases. Once we secured the evidence that was favorable to the defense, I filed a request for expert witness. You're shocked that the government denied it; their stated basis essentially challenged the weight the evidence would provide.

After litigating the issue, the military judge announced on the record that we had met and exceeded the necessity standard to compel our expert witness in digital forensics. In fact, he announced to the uniformed counsel present that they should take note of my proficiency in this matter and keep a copy of my motion handy for their future reference and use.

In addition to the data regarding her respiration, heart rate, and sleep, we wanted this evidence introduced to challenge the notion of when and how Major LeDoux would have gotten access to amphetamines. A huge component of every case analysis that I perform is to always be cognizant of the steps I would take on a given case were I the prosecuting attorney. I served as a military prosecutor for more than four years, training junior prosecutors, and prosecutors from other military branches on complex litigation. When I put on my prosecutor hat, I ask what are the things that the government should have done in a given case?

This case was no different. They had no evidence that Joann had access to Adderall® or other amphetamines. True to my expectations, they merely insinuated that she was a nurse and must have been able to get them. Through a series of witnesses, I put to bed the idea that military hospitals are raining amphetamines or that providers are sharing stashes of Adderall®.

I also introduced evidence that allowed me to argue that based on her knowledge of medicine, Joann could have obtained a valid prescription for Adderall® if she wanted. She did not want big pharma solutions; this was the entire reason she turned to the promises of this corporation who had been advertising on her Instagram® feed.

The reason I felt a heightened level of stress on this case was because it was not just my client's military career and nursing / anesthesia provider license that was at stake. Inexplicably to me, Joann's divorce lawyer made her custody of her children contingent on her remaining in the military. If she left the service, her kids moved to the primary custody of her ex-husband, and if she wanted to exercise any parenting time, she would have to move to where he was living to be near to her children. On the east coast.

I am a mom; and I mom hard for my four small humans. I laid down each night to attempt sleep, considering her worry about not having her babies with her. I woke up each morning during the trial, and I promptly went to the toilet to vomit from the stress of it all. Eating to maintain any calories was a difficult task. My appetite vanished with worry for her and her angels.

By the time of trial, the government's case boiled down to a handful of witnesses who would attest to the collection of Major LeDoux's sample and introducing the results of the urine's testing. That's really all they had. Among them were the observer who watched her pee in the cup; the person who filled out the paperwork and packaged it for the unit; the person from the base office who then packaged it up to send it to the lab; and the lab's testifying expert.

We put on 21 witnesses. The first group I can classify as people who saw her that day who said she was not acting peculiarly, not acting out of her norm, and not anxious to provide a sample.

The second grouping was a parade of character witnesses to talk about her good military character, her character for truthfulness, and also her devotion as a mother. The third group were the foundational science witnesses and the experts.

Joann also testified under oath that she didn't knowingly consume amphetamines. She explained all of the steps she had taken upon learning of the testing results and the entire process to try to find the truth of why her sample had tested positive. In a rare move, I had Joann testify as the defense's first witness. No one was expecting that.

When criminal defendants testify, it is often last or at least sandwiched between other witnesses the defense knows will be strong. Never first. But who needs to follow "rules" when you have strategy and experience. The cross-examination did not leave any nicks in the armor of Joann's truth.

One of the more troubling moves by the government in this case came during their cross examination of Joann's commander. We called him as a defense witness to testify about Major LeDoux's reaction to being notified of this positive urinalysis. He said her reaction was just utter shock, without a doubt, utter astonishment when she was notified of the positive result. I also questioned him about whether he was aware of any efforts by military law enforcement to learn about Major LeDoux's behavior in the weeks leading up to the "failed" test. This was to highlight how poor this investigation had been. The commander attested that nobody from law enforcement had interviewed him and that nobody from law enforcement coordinated interviews of anybody else in the organization, at least not through him.

During the prosecutor's cross-examination of the commander, she attacks his credibility. The gestalt of her examination was that just because he didn't have any personal knowledge of law enforcement coordinating interviews, doesn't mean they didn't happen. Understand that the reason this line of questioning is so inappropriate is because this prosecutor *knew* that no investigation happened. This prosecutor *knew* that no investigator came down to the unit. This prosecutor *knew* that no one from the unit was questioned.

As I am watching this unfold, I'm sitting there grievously offended as a former prosecutor. A prosecutor cannot mislead or try to draw an inference or even insinuate that a fact is true that she knows is not true.

What an incredibly improper move, not only for ethics reasons but also as a poor tactical consideration. After the prosecutor cross-examined the commander, I called multiple witnesses who were nurse anesthesia providers to attest that no one had come to question them. One of the more senior providers made several panel members smile at the corners of their mouths when we went into a bit more detail. I asked words to the effect of "Do you think you would know if the investigators had come down to the unit to ask around?" Oh, absolutely. He said, "look, nurses gossip, we gossip. We would've all heard if someone came over or called the chief of the anesthesia department." Did anybody from law enforcement come over? No.

For the nail in the proverbial coffin, I next called their investigator to the stand. I asked him whether he went to the unit to ask around. He testified that he had not, and that no one had. When this answer landed, I looked over at the prosecutor. Well, we can say look; glare would be more accurate. Then I looked at the panel. They did not look pleased.

Military court-martial panel members typically have the minimum of a master's degree; they're quick, they get it. And when you try to play fast and loose with the truth, you lose your credibility.

After my client testified, I asked the military judge to introduce into evidence the sworn statement Major LeDoux had given to law enforcement. I offered specific portions of the statement as exclusions to hearsay as prior consistent statements. And I offered the entire statement for what's called a non-hearsay purpose so that the panel could review it and assess whether the government's decision that no investigative steps needed to be taken.

The same prosecutor who was insinuating untruths stands up to oppose me offering Joann's prior statement. She says that she thinks I'm trying to sneak evidence before the panel improperly. Seriously.

Before I even had the opportunity to start defending myself, the judge showed that he had my back. And he said, "I know you did not just mean to say what it very much sounded like you just said." Let's be clear that this was not the first time and I'm sure certainly won't be the last that I'm dealing with prosecutors who are themselves committing infractions and yet are trying to cast dispersions on me.

The military judge said, "she literally just asked for a limiting instruction about the non-hearsay purpose for which the statement should be considered," which fundamentally means that I am not trying to sneak in anything. I articulated a theory of relevance and a hearsay exclusion.

Now ultimately, he did not admit the entire statement for the panel to consider. He performed what we call an evidentiary balancing test. And I can't disagree with his analysis or ruling.

But the judge also determined that I was able to introduce parts of her prior statement for their truth and consistency. This is the hearsay exclusion. Again, this is chess, not checkers, people; chess, not checkers.

While I cannot scientifically prove that the supplements Major LeDoux took were adulterated, whether intentionally or otherwise, I am firmly convinced they are to blame for her positive urinalysis. The CEO from the corporation who sold the supplements had to admit under oath that his company does not screen their ingredients for amphetamines, and neither do his suppliers. Pretty scary stuff, particularly since we are also confident the ingredients are coming from questionable overseas sources. The CEO hired his own lawyer to help him refuse to answer any questions pertaining to "trademark secrets." He did not want to disclose where he obtains his ingredients. Red flag, much?

The CEO also acknowledged that one of his Instagram® ads pronounced his product as "the all-natural alternative to Adderall®." I mean, really. I thought the company had pulled that ad and questioned him on it during his examination. No, he insisted – it is still an active advertisement; it is one of their "best ads." Seriously.

After about two hours and 20 minutes of deliberations, the panel came back and announced they had found Joann not guilty. After the judge dismissed the panel, she broke down, and she could not stop crying. I was numb.

My client will get to stay in service. My client hopefully will get to shed this from her reputation. My client will be able to keep her kids. We'll see what happens with that prosecutor. We'll also see what happens with the civil suit I would like to file against the ingredient suppliers, the packagers, the producers, and anyone else connected to the product.

It took me more than a couple weeks to return to a semi normal diet and some level of normal sleep for me.

These cases are never easy, particularly when the stakes are so incredibly high. I remain indebted to Joann LeDoux for believing in me and staying the course of my strategy. I remain indebted to her, despite the personal struggles we faced together in this case, for finding me and allowing me to stand up with her, for her, and next to her. I am honored to count her as a lifetime friend.

Chapter 11

TRUTH SMACKS YOU IN THE FACE

She thought her fake tears would make me relent, retreat, or recoil. No way.

My cross-examination of the poor child would last only about a half hour or so. She was only eight by the time she would testify. And highlighting the impossibility of her perceptions, the reality that she had been manipulated to believe that she had been abused would not take very long.

Her mother required more. The judge took a recess during the nearly eight hours that I cross-examined mom to ask did I believe I was really getting anything helpful. I did, and I said as much. He let me continue.

She eventually figured out that leaning forward to throw her arms and torso down on the witness box would not make me stop. I merely walked over to counsel table to take a sip of hot tea or water. I would wait for her to sort of sheepishly look up to see where I had gone. And then I would continue. At one point, I believe I even asked the judge if I could sit down during the pauses in testimony. I mean, heels, people.

My client, Lieutenant Colonel Michael G, had briefed me that this was how she habitually behaved in family court. Only there, they did not have time to wait her out.

I did. I had all the patience in the world.

From this case, I confirm there is evil in the world. Sometimes evil presents itself because a person is immoral; in this case, I classify her up as amoral. She is outside the world of morality, and I can attribute it to mental illness. But I also believe that she knows that she is lying.

What I believe she exhibited is a form of Munchausen's Syndrome by proxy. She seemed to feel the need to create danger and trauma in the mind of her child so that her child would need to be rescued by her. This elevates her position, makes her not just important, but all knowing and the lone voice to ensuring her children were "safe."

And she made up every detail. And then fed them to her second youngest child, who was psychologically the most vulnerable and impressionable. At an age where memory is malleable, and she was nearly the most suggestible of her children. Did I mention she has a master's degree in elementary education and learning?

When the child was questioned the first time by a forensic interviewer, she made no disclosures. Everything with her daddy was great; she was confused by the questions. By the time she went in for her second interview, she was holding onto a piece of paper that her mommy told her she should bring with her because she had forgotten to tell them things the last time. The paper would help her remember.

You can't make this up.

As the daughter tried to recount what she was alleging as her experience, the allegations lacked indications that she lived these moments. There was no sensory detail, no context, and no appreciation for what those supposed events would have been like.

Yes, children have limitations in their understanding and also in their ability to articulate. But forensic interview techniques take these constraints into consideration in evaluating claims. Or at least they are supposed to.

Anyone watching these videos could see the coaching. It was staggering really. And yet the government held Lieutenant Colonel Michael G hostage by the claims.

As the case progressed, every time I applied pressure points, the divorcing spouse came forward to report that the rest of the children were also making disclosures.

There were constant continuances while the government investigated the latest claims.

I recall that the greatest wave of new accusations came after the divorcing spouse failed to show for a motions hearing where her presence was demanded by my written filing.

When a party drafts and files a written prayer for relief, known as a motion, procedure requires its author to outline evidence the pleading relies on and to list any witnesses to be produced for testimony during the litigation. We had listed the divorcing spouse, the mother of the child complainant, as a witness necessary for testifying regarding essential facts to the defense motion. The government did not object, which means they were agreeing to produce her.

The morning of that round of pretrial litigation, we learned that she did not bother to show for the hearing. We were paralyzed from litigating that issue, and I was furious. This woman had a knack for derailing process, at least when it seemingly benefitted her.

During trial, I believe the clock demonstrated I spent more than eight hours with her on the stand. Most of that time was her histrionic fake tears, throwing herself down on the witness stand's desk like platform in front of where she sat.

When I leaned over to ask Michael if this was typical, he shared that this was precisely what had transpired in family court, and that the civilian judges would pass on the matter and carry things over to a later date.

Her antics were likewise making his divorce and custody cases impossible to resolve. I offered that she would not be able to escape my questions in this way.

After several hours of watching the adult witness behave like a temper-throwing toddler, the military judge halfheartedly explained that he was not deriving much information from the examination. That was kind of my point. I insisted we continue, and he did not try to stop me.

Between her fake sobs, during those hot tea or water breaks, my back was even partially facing the witness at times.

I needed to send a message to all concerned that I was not moved by her false emotion, and that I would not be deterred in my questioning.

By contrast, my examination of Michael's eight-year old child was quite short. And her experience was far less uncomfortable.

There is no reason to cause additional trauma to a child who testifies. Do not be confused – I am not saying this child suffered any trauma by her father. But being made to believe that her father committed horrific acts on her is itself a trauma. I was not going to add to her mother's sins.

We built rapport as we began our dialogue, and she leaned back in her chair, at times even smiling at me. She knew that I wanted to hear what she would tell me. That builds trust, and for this little girl who was being used as a pawn, it was critical for her to see me as someone who valued her voice.

There is this sense that criminal defense attorneys want to shred every witness in cross-examination. Perhaps that is the practice for some; that is not mine. As I had prepared for this questioning, I had the benefit of superb expert assistance: Dr. Mark Chambers. He had taken me through all of the issues that he saw in the child's disclosures. One of the most salient points I needed to hit home was that her memories were false; the way to demonstrate that they were false was to emphasize their limitations and how they felt to the child. For example, she recounted on the stand for the first time that she could recall her dad touching her "over her diaper." Children do not wear diapers past a stage in their development within which they can have trustworthy recollections. She was convinced the event had happened, but it could not have given the age she would have been while wearing diapers.

I will spare more details about the nature of the complaint, lest I lose every reader. It is sometimes quite easy to forget how dark this world that my professional world has inhabited for the last two decades.

On a business trip among other Army Special Victim Prosecutors in 2010, every person not in our group who was within unfortunate earshot of our discussion and banter about cases moved to the other side of a tour boat. Had they moved any faster, we might have tipped. Only one in our number noticed, and then he alerted us to our transgressions.

Lieutenant Colonel G's case was a rare one where I advised my client to select judge alone for his forum choice. I have only given this advice in a handful of cases in the past twenty years of litigating military courts-martial. My default advice is to choose a jury of all

Officers, even when the client is an enlisted person. In this particular case, I told Michael that I believed justice would be served by having Colonel Timothy Hayes preside over his case as the finder of fact, and if any finding of guilty was made, to also be his sentencing authority.

I first met (then) Major Hayes when I was Captain Stewart, and we were both serving at Fort Hood, Texas in 2008. Tim was leaving the position of senior defense counsel as I was arriving from Germany to start my second consecutive year of military court-martial defense as a uniformed counsel. It just so happened that Tim had a client who was an Army warrant officer who had gone through an investigation for allegations of child sexual misconduct with his stepdaughter and biological daughter.

I'll spare additional details of that troubling case. I can offer that the first investigation concluded without charging. It was not until additional allegations surfaced several months later, after Tim left his position in the defense world, that the warrant officer was charged. I was assigned the case for the same client that Tim had previously represented for the investigation. Tim had transitioned from senior defense counsel to being a military judge on the same installation. I advised that client to make a request for Tim to be assigned to his case because he had represented him for the same underlying conduct. Honestly, I did not expect the trial judiciary to approve this request, known as an Individual Military Counsel request or IMC, for short. I halfheartedly thought it might be a decent appellate issue if they denied the IMC. They did not. Tim was not happy, but *c'est la vie…*

The shared trauma Tim and I suffered from that case, the most egregious case I had experienced at that point in my career, helped me to know that Tim was the exact right person to sit in judgment of Michael's trial. Tim knew what an actual child sexual abuser looked and acted like, and he would know that Michael was anything but.

I will never forget the look on the Judge Hayes' face when he came out after deliberating to announce his verdict.

At least seven different times during the trial, the government prosecutors had attempted to introduce the child's second of the two forensic interviews into evidence. Substantively, as evidence of the criminal misconduct. Yeah, that doesn't work in military court. It is at its most basic level inadmissible hearsay. Courts favor the "crucible of cross-examination," and out-of-court statements are for the most part deemed unreliable and therefore inadmissible. Each time, the prosecutors made their argument, I was able to defeat it, but I offered a reason for which the judge should consider the video.

After Dr. Chambers testified as our defense expert witness to comment about what issues he identified in the disclosures the child had made, I acknowledged to the Court that one non-hearsay purpose for the Court to consider both of the forensic interviews would be to use them to evaluate Dr. Chambers' testimony. Dr. Chambers' expert opinion relied heavily on what he observed in those interviews, and it would be an important way for the judge to assess Dr. Chambers' observations, opinions, and overall credibility.

It appeared the judge was growing as annoyed by the government's continued efforts to introduce the interviews substantively as I was, and he announced that when he went back to deliberate that he would review the videos. He explained that if, during the course of his watching them, he determined that there was a viable evidentiary avenue to consider the interviews substantively, he would come out and reconvene the Court to allow me to be heard on the matter. He explained that he would consider the video interviews for the limited purpose that I had posited for assessing the expert testimony.

Judge Hayes deliberated about 10 minutes longer than the videos took to play. I kept track. When we filed back into Court, I could feel the usual tension in the room, but it was amplified. I didn't feel nervous, but I didn't feel exactly confident either. I am certain I was exhausted.

Typically, trial prep and the trial litigation knock me on my keester, emotionally. It is hard to describe how every cell of me is required to focus, anticipate, strategize, and evaluate each question, answer, and move while court is in session. If one were able to capture the running news ticker of thoughts and considerations moving through my brain, it would be busier than the feeds of major news channels. Combined.

Do you know in movies when a person becomes hyper-focused on one person or event and the others blur to the back, and cinematographers will sometimes quiet all other noise?

Yeah, it is nothing like that. Nothing is blurred, nothing is quieted, but you have to be focused on all details, all broad pictures, and larger over-arching themes.

At once.
It. Is. Exhausting.

By the time that deliberations begin, I can feel a mix of relief and vigilance. Sometimes the scale tips to one side of that spectrum, and I recall this case presenting almost squarely down the middle of that balance.

Judge Timothy Hayes waited at least thirty seconds after sitting down on the bench before he called the court to order. He wasn't shuffling papers or trying to pull up notes on his computer. He was glaring. At the prosecutors. I mean, full on, death stare. And he meant it.

Michael glanced over to me for reassurance. I clenched a fist in support under the table between us.

When the words "accused and defense counsel, please rise" finally left his mouth and we rose to face judgment, I knew what the verdict would be. Not guilty to all charges and their specifications.

We call that a "win." Mostly.

But in these scenarios, who really wins? Not Michael, whose relationship with his kids was splintered if not shattered by their mom's mental illness, hate, and lies. Not the child who testified, in full belief that these events had occurred. Not the other children who may also believe abuse happened. Certainly not the system that is charged with ensuring that only righteous cases are brought forward.

Years after Michael's military case had resolved I learned that his children's mother made more allegations when he was retiring. She just would not stop.

When a separate client took his own life more than a year after his full acquittal, it shook me. I reached out to Michael and many others to check on their wellbeing, to reassure them that they were never alone, and that their place in the world mattered. He was grateful and echoed that he knew that I deeply care for my clients.

There is no greater calling than the one I get to wake up to every day. While the facts of each case vary, the spirit of those who choose me as their advocate and whose cases I choose to champion have a consistent thread that runs through them: honor. Each one volunteered to serve, and while some make more of their opportunities than others, those who sit next to me at counsel table become the family I choose.

I pray that someday now retired Lieutenant Colonel Michael G's kids will know the superb man and father that

I know. And that years of therapy can bridge the gap that has been made into a chasm by those in a system who have failed all concerned.

Jocelyn C. Stewart

Chapter 12

A FUNERAL WOULD HAVE BEEN BETTER

One of the biggest regrets of my life was losing his case. I almost did not recover. Almost.

I was ready to hang up my spurs as a cowgirl litigator. I really was.

Reliving this case even in this context is taxing on me emotionally. There's a reason it is my last chapter, and there is a reason it is the last chapter I am completing.

But it is a story that must be told. If I only recounted the cases where a factually innocent client was acquitted, that would not move the needle in why military justice reform is absolutely necessary. Hint: the reform we need is not the kind that has been occurring since 2007.

Being present for the sentencing proceedings in his case was worse than any funeral I have ever attended, have avoided attending, or will avoid attending in years to come.

Somewhere in the neighborhood of thirty green berets showed up in dress uniform for the occasion. I felt I had failed every one of them, and my client in particular. I have relived every tactical decision I made prior to the case and those I made during the trial, in a constant loop.

After the verdict came back guilty to the "lesser included" offense that the judge instructed the panel on over my objection, something in me broke.

This was the first Article 120 case that I defended *as a civilian* practitioner, having left active duty months before. I was still stepping into my role as independent from the role of uniformed counsel, and I see my biggest failing as not doing more to stop the judge from the antics he pulled. Or at least doing more to try.

At one point during the trial, I had to fight back the words to ask him if he would please remove his judicial robe to join the prosecutors at counsel table, rather than continuing to pretend to be a neutral arbiter. Honestly, I wish I would have said that on the record. Perhaps that might have stopped the runaway boulders that I was having to dodge from the bench.

Even as I type that, it feels like hollow excuses. As in sports, ultimately it is the coach who bears ultimate responsibility. I don't mean to shirk that – as lead counsel, everything falls on me. Everything.

We had substantial evidence that the complainant had embellished her reaction to the supposed assault. She testified during the Article 32(b) investigation when those actually existed in their old form. She alleged that she had not left her apartment for weeks because of how devastated she was after the "assault." We had photographs and social media posts indicating she was out partying. But because she was apparently in the company of men, the military judge excluded that evidence pursuant to Military Rule of Evidence 412. Protect the "victim." Give me a break.

In this trial, I also broke a cardinal rule that I did not really process as a cardinal rule until after this loss: I went to trial without having a verbatim transcript of the prior statements of the alleging victim. I caution counsel against this misstep every chance I get.

For slippery witnesses, and always for the complaining witness, you must have the transcript to be able to successfully impeach them.

To impeach means to confront with prior inconsistencies or to impeach with implausibility or contradictions that exist from other evidence or witnesses. Impeachment is the bread and butter for any trial litigator, and going into trial without the transcripts is like forgetting the butter knife. You might be able to spread something while fumbling with your fingers, but it sure isn't going to be pretty. And it won't be nearly as neat.

Even still, the charging decision should have saved us from any risk of conviction. Often junior prosecutors draft the charging instrument marked with poor choices among a litany of options, and in some cases, they downright get it impossibly wrong. The miliary has largely divested itself of its experienced litigators, so supervisory prosecutors don't know much more than their underlings in guiding them on the choices they have.

This was one of those cases that should have been the latter – the one where they can't possibly prove what was on the charge sheet because they chose the wrong kind of charge. As a former prosecutor, when I review a charging decision, I ask myself what I would have charged. It is seldom what I see staring back at me.

When we turned to the topic of instructions, the judge stepped in, pencil whipped a new specification, and called it a lesser included offense. I nearly lost my mind.

A lesser included offense can only go to the jury for their deliberations and vote if it truly has already been fairly noticed on the charge sheet for the defense to adequately prepare. There is a session on the record devoted to a discussion of the instructions that a military panel will receive to help them understand the standards, definitions, elements, and defenses. Part of the dialogue on the record with the judge is a part where the judge asks whether either side believes that any lesser included offenses have been reasonably raised or requests instruction on a lesser included offense.

During this trial's session about instructions, the judge dutifully followed the script and asked the prosecution and defense did we see any lesser included offenses.

This is always an interesting moment, because I promise you the Army prosecutors almost never have even thought about what instructions they believe should be given. It is always an afterthought, never a part of deliberate planning or strategy. They often don't know to even fumble to find the Instructions Checklist at the back of Department of the Army Pamphlet 27-9. It's mighty helpful, and hint: it is even more helpful to case preparation when used at the outset.

The prosecutors in this case responded to the judge's question and said no, they did not see any lesser included offenses. I likewise told the judge that we did not see any.

Then the military judge starts explaining that he did. When he announced new language for a specification that he had created and starts calling out the exact verbiage, a big part of me knew that there was probably going to be a guilty finding.

To this one specification that the judge had just made up. After watching the trial and morphing his "charge" to meet the evidence.

He wanted a conviction, and he got it.

There were several moments during this trial when I felt like I was present but not really.

Some might call it disassociation, and in the rear view mirror that his hindsight, I would have to concur.

When you put the pressure on yourself that I do on me, to win every time, anticipating that you are going to fail is itself a slow funeral.

Eric was there alongside me in the moments when I went into labor with my fourth child. As a Special Forces medic, he tried to spring into action to help in any way that he could. I say tried because I wouldn't let him.

Through contractions and some stifled laughter, I asked him did he think he needed to boil water? I can still see his giant smile. And his dimples.

Eric showed genuine concern for my health and the health of my baby-to-be, and he didn't care that we were in the middle of his Article 32(b) investigation. Think preliminary hearing but with more teeth and rights.

When I was working Eric's case in preparation for motions and the trial, I was again a new mom, and I was up at various hours of the night to care for my infant. I would file motions or send emails randomly at 2am or so because that's when I was awake, and the house was still and quiet. In those days, I had a home office only, and would meet perspective clients at a nearby coffee shop.

I blind copied Eric on the emails and pleadings I sent. He told me that I "slept like a Ranger." He also told me that when a person graduates Ranger school, it just means they are good at walking.

Those memories still make me smile, just slightly.

Only just slightly because I feel like I ruined his life. I know that I did not, and what's more, I know that he doesn't see it that way. But it is hard to forgive imperfection when you've been a perfectionist for most of your life. I try to tell myself I am in recovery from perfectionism, but most days that isn't the candid truth. It's hard to shed that from yourself completely when it's been stitched into your soul like the rough threads in burlap.

Remember that funeral? Yeah, the one with all the green berets showing up in solidarity and support? We didn't make the situation any better when we achieved such a low sentence that Eric's case did not receive a direct appeal in the military's appellate system. Eric's military record and good military character were unsurpassed.

In fact during the trial, the defense tried to introduce evidence of Eric's impeccable military character to demonstrate the tendency of his innocence to the charges. "Military Justice Reform" now makes that impossible for select charges, including all offenses of a sexual nature. But in 2013 when this case was going to trial, we were still operating under the rule that would permit it.

There are many ways of achieving this goal of introducing character evidence. One is to call witnesses to attest to their opinion or knowledge of the reputation of the person's good military character; another is to introduce character affidavits. Lastly, a less often used method is to introduce documents from the client's service record. This last category has a fairly wide caveat in that you cannot run afoul of the overarching rule to not introduce specific instances of behavior when dealing with character evidence.

Always trying to teach, I explained this nuance to the uniformed counsel who was assigned to represent Eric with me. I told him to prepare two sets of the exhibits: one with the specific instances in case the prosecutors did not object; and one that was redacted of the specific instances of conduct in case they did, or the judge imposed himself on the process.

I assigned the military counsel the role of standing to address the Court to offer the first version of the exhibit. When he did, the military judge sneered at him and openly showed disgust to the counsel, dressing him down and mocking him. All in front of the panel.

We were both caught off guard, particularly since the rule itself lists service records as a viable method for introducing character. I can say that it is not often if ever used in Army cases and is far more common in Air Force trials. I practice in all service courts, and I believe the depth of my knowledge is made more robust by being exposed to the differences among the varying service courts.

Clearly, the judge had not been exposed to this part of the rule in his practice.

Despite him dressing us down in front of the panel, the mark of unprofessional conduct, we circled back to the issue. I quickly jumped onto the LEXIS-NEXIS® search engine and found a military case that demonstrated it was a permissible method for introducing character evidence. I asked the judge in an almost saccharine voice if we could please have an "802."

Rule for Court-Martial 802 outlines the ability for the military judge to meet with counsel off the record to discuss logistics, the way-ahead, and other administrative matters, provided these matters are all fairly captured and summarized on the record at the next open session of the Court.

Not wanting to draw the Court's ego-ridden ire, I had written the case citation on a sticky note. As we filed back into his chambers, I respectfully asked if he would please review the case citation and permit us to ask for reconsideration. He all but snatched the paper from my hand.

More than twenty minutes later he filed back into Court. He then read aloud a ruling that he acknowledged that the rule would ordinarily permit introduction of character evidence in this manner, but that he was inserting a balancing test under Military Rule of Evidence 403, that the evidence was needlessly cumulative with other evidence introduced regarding character.

It was a bullshit ruling, but he was quite proud of himself.

I know this because after the trial, the judge was conducting a "bridge the gap" session with the military attorneys, and I just so happened to arrive in time to hear the aftermath of the judge mocking my efforts on the request for reconsideration.

As a civilian practitioner, I generally will not attend these post trial rap sessions with the judge. In nearly all cases, I sit through watching the judge coach the prosecutor in how to do his job better next time, and I am not here for that. I am not a prosecutor, and I have no desire to train them or to watch it happen. It boils my blood. These sessions are supposed to provide general feedback about trial advocacy skills for both sides, but that is not how the majority of judges treat these opportunities. In one trial I told the judge I would not attend anymore of his 802 sessions because I would not sit back and watch him coach and mentor the prosecutor about how to convict my client. If I am not there, the judge can't hold an 802 session. The same would be true for a "Bridge the Gap" but the judge has the authority to order the military counsel to be present. But not me. So, I skip them. And candidly, I encourage all military defense counsel to avoid them; the judge can't coach the prosecutors if they aren't there too.

As part of pretrial litigation in this trial, we had received sealed medical records of the complaining witness. There was a significant protective order surrounding the records, and I was directed to provide my paper copy back to the Court. This was the only reason I was returning to the courtroom, and specifically to the judge's chambers. I did not want to give this fella any reason to find I had violated his order, lest he later try to hold me in contempt.

As I walked up, I knocked and entered. Silence stifled laughter, and I knew at once the laughs had been at my expense. You know, those awkward moments when you walk up to a group who suddenly stops talking at once. Yeah, they had just been talking about me.

I explained the reason for my return, handed over the sealed documents, and exited once more.

The uniformed defense counsel would later explain that I had been correct – the judge was making fun of my efforts at reconsideration on the service records. He said that I had made a significant strategic error by giving the judge the opportunity to fix his mistake, and gosh golly, hadn't he been so cleaver to find a way to still keep out the evidence. I calmly explained to the uniformed counsel that as trial attorneys we always want to win at trial. This was not a significant enough issue to sit on it and have it translate to any post-trial relief. It wouldn't have made a difference to the appellate court, but perhaps these service records would have mattered to our panel.

It wasn't about justice for this judge. He was about securing Eric's conviction and maintaining the esteem he saw himself as deserving.

He was abusing his power. This same judge's later ousting post military retirement as the second most senior county attorney in Thurston County, Washington would confirm as much.

Eric received two rank reductions and 60 days confinement. This means that his case would never be reviewed by the Army Court of Criminal Appeals. At least, not unless the issue was certified to it by the Judge Advocate General of the Army. Hint: we tried that too.

Since Eric's case and only this year, in fact, there is a new rule that will require an automatic appeal for any conviction that carries with it the secondary consequence of making the military accused a registered sex offender. It does little to help Eric, but maybe it will help someone else.

The heartache I feel in retelling Eric's case should not reverse the pride I know I should feel that he chose me to stand up for him as his lawyer and more importantly as someone with a deep, sincere caring for his wellbeing.

I am in awe every day for the feats of heroism and dedication that marks the character and actions of my clients. That Eric must walk through life having himself been the true victim of a system with more shortcomings than could fill this book, is tragic. As my heart vacillates between pride and shame, I'll do my best to teeter back to pride as often as I can.

To do otherwise would insult the sacrifice of service that Eric made for his country and before the unfortunate altar that is the military's [in]justice system. I think a part of me has been trying to make up for it ever since, and certainly will fuel me for the foreseeable future.

Chapter 13

"HAS BEEN"?

There was a time not so long ago when I was questioning whether I could persist in the field of military [in]justice for much longer. Carrying the weight of these cases and more importantly of these fine people asks a lot. Some days, I tend to believe it requires too much. Even the "victories" and sometimes particularly the victories.

Compassion fatigue, vicarious trauma, whatever term you wish to use. It is real. And it can be crushing.

Stepping back in time to memorialize these triumphs and other case "war stories" in my TikTok videos has been important to my journey. And to my longevity in this industry.

The title of the book "It *Has Been* My Honor" suggests at least in part that this career I've made is coming to an end.

In some ways this signaling *has been* intentional.

Now on the other side of retirement from the military, it seems natural to be pondering whether I want additional change. Are there pivots I am entertaining that are drawing my energy and attention? There are.

Reaching back out to the service members depicted in this book has reminded me, however, that my lawyer work isn't finished. How that looks precisely remains undecided.

I'll stay for as long as I am able, in cases and on behalf of individuals for whom I feel called to serve. But as I have explained at the outset of this project, I am seeking opportunities that have ripple effects and can course correct to impact many more than any individual client or case.

In the last year, I have found gratitude for using social media platforms that bring a voice to those whom a system would otherwise silence. I will keep leveraging outreach opportunities to educate service members about availing them of their rights. I want to ensure the machine levied against them will not seem insurmountable. I will continue my efforts to teach practitioners to form an "army" of dedicated advocates who want to ensure the legacy of the military will not be left to those with partisan agendas.

No matter which projects I choose, at the helm will always be my focus of military justice reform. The system must be re-shaped by those who know, understand, and live these cases. The military cannot keep turning their backs on those who have answered the call to serve our nation.

Ensuring that service members are not left to the peril of politics will continue to be my honor.

About The Author

Jocelyn C. Stewart attended Louisiana's designated honors college, the Louisiana Scholars' College, in Natchitoches, Louisiana from 1996 to 2000. After being awarded a three-year ROTC cadet scholarship and a scholarship from the honors college, she graduated first in her class of honors students, summa cum laude, and "with highest distinction." Ms. Stewart commissioned Distinguished Military Graduate from Northwestern State University's Demon Battalion as a Second Lieutenant in Military Intelligence. She was selected to attend law school as an educational delay student from 2000 – 2003.

Since Jocelyn graduated law school from the Paul M. Hebert Law Center at Louisiana State University in 2003, she has exclusively practiced military law.

An active duty Army JAG Corps from early 2004 until late 2012, Ms. Stewart worked in uniform for more than seven years in court-martial practice. Her initial assignment was as a legal assistance attorney and a Part Time Military Magistrate where she reviewed law enforcement applications for search and/or seizure authorizations and command decisions to place servicemembers in pretrial confinement pending their courts-martial.

In 2005, Jocelyn became a "trial counsel," serving as the command's legal advisor in military justice matters and prosecuting any of its Soldiers facing military criminal trial. After serving as trial counsel for just over 2 years, Jocelyn fought to stay in the courtroom.

In 2007, she took over as a trial defense counsel at Wiesbaden Army Air Field (WAAF), Germany. In 2008, she moved to the then busiest court-martial jurisdiction of any of the services: Fort Hood, Texas. From 2008 until 2010, Jocelyn defended multiple high profile cases including premeditated murder, the kidnapping of a two-day old infant from the base hospital, and a Soldier who staged his own "kidnapping" by members of the Mexican cartel.

In 2012, Jocelyn was hand-selected to stay in a courtroom advocate role and fill one of the first Special Victim Prosecutor positions. Responsible for the Midwest region, Ms. Stewart handled all "special victim" cases for Fort Riley, Fort Leavenworth, and Fort McCoy. A "special victim" case is defined as any allegation of adult sexual assault by a civilian or a military member, any allegation of child sexual abuse or molestation, all allegations of intimate partner violence, and those with evidence of digital exploitation of children. For two years, Jocelyn headed and oversaw the prosecutions of more than sixty special victim cases.

As a Special Victim Prosecutor (SVP), she achieved the first two non-homicide life without parole sentences in the Army's history. In addition to the supportive and instructive role she played in the courtroom for the junior trial counsel in her region, Ms. Stewart's job as SVP included extensive travel to teach prosecution techniques to trial counsel of all branches of service.

In 2012, Jocelyn left active service to pursue a practice dedicated to defending servicemembers worldwide, with particular emphasis in sexual assault investigations and sexual assault court-martial defense. As a civilian court-martial specialist, she has represented clients across the United States and overseas, from the west coast to the east coast, the gulf coast, and the Midwest. Her clients serve the Army, the Air Force, the Navy, the Marine Corps, the Coast Guard, and even the Space Force.

After a three-year break in service to focus on building her civilian court-martial practice, in late September 2015,

Jocelyn assessed into the reserve component of the Army JAGC. She first served for more than fifteen months as the Anchorage Team Leader of the 6th Legal Operations Detachment (LOD). She also served as the 6th LOD's Public Affairs Officer.

In January 2017, Jocelyn joined the adjunct faculty of the Criminal law department of The Judge Advocate Generals Legal Center and School. In recent memory, Jocelyn was the first defense attorney selected to join the faculty, which historically has consisted of federal prosecutors. After competing with dozens of applicants and undergoing a thorough screening and interview process, Jocelyn was invited to join the faculty. During her three-year adjunct faculty tenure, Jocelyn taught hundreds of RC / AC Judge Advocates about UCMJ criminal case updates during the 2018 Western Reserve On-Site. She has also taught nearly one hundred trial counsel and defense counsel at the Intermediate Trial Advocate Course (ITAC) in several iterations of the course.

Lastly, Jocelyn taught two separate iterations of TJAGLCS LLM graduate students about military motions practice and graded multiple LLM graduate course final papers. Ms. Stewart's tenure on the Criminal law faculty ended effective January 9, 2020.

In 2021 and 2022, Jocelyn was invited to instruct dozens of uniformed defense counsel at a Defense Counsel Assistance Program (DCAP) conference held in Arizona. She teaches for several days on topics including motions writing and litigation in military practice. She also teaches counsel about resilience in litigation, how to work with civilian counsel, and overall strategies in serving as a defense counsel in military court-martial practice.

In 2021, Jocelyn also was promoted to the rank of Lieutenant Colonel in the Reserve Component. She is retired from the reserve component on April 4, 2023.

Ms. Stewart can be reached through her firm at:
www.UCMJ-Defender.com

Other Books By The Author

JOCELYN C. STEWART, ESQ.

SHAPING THE
BATTLEFIELD

**HOW TO DRAFT MOTIONS
IN MILITARY PRACTICE**

Foreword by: LtCol (Retired) Brendon Tukey

JOCELYN C. STEWART, ESQ.

SHAPING THE
BATTLEFIELD II

**HOW TO LITIGATE MOTIONS
IN MILITARY PRACTICE**

Foreword by: Colonel (Retired) Jeffery R. Nance

JOCELYN C. STEWART, ESQ.

SHAPING THE
BATTLEFIELD III

**RULE 412 MOTIONS
IN MILITARY PRACTICE**

Foreword by: LTC (Ret) Sean F. Mangan

MILITARY COURT RULES
OF THE UNITED STATES

PROCEDURE, CITATION,
PROFESSIONAL RESPONSIBILITY,
CIVILITY, AND JUDICIAL CONDUCT

EIGHTH EDITION

Benjamin K. Grimes
Eugene R. Fidell
Franklin D. Rosenblatt
Jonathan F. Potter
Jocelyn C. Stewart,
Editors

2022

LexisNexis

Order copies at: https://www.ucmj-defender.com/resources/

Jocelyn C. Stewart

About The Firm

Unlike many of her competitors, the Law Office of Jocelyn C Stewart, Corp. focuses from day one at running a collateral investigation to understand the state of the government's evidence and to attempt to find evidence the government has yet to uncover. The firm's ability to make the most significant impact is linked to how early clients find us. Investigation is the most important aspect of any case preparation and in many cases, is the best opportunity to stop a case before the preferral stage. However tempted a service member may be to "wait and see what happens" most often it is a mistake to wait.

Don't wait; contact the firm today.

Law Office of JOCELYN C. STEWART
1201 Pacific Avenue
Suite 600
Tacoma, WA 98402
Office: 253-212-6940
www.ucmj-defender.com

www.ingramcontent.com/pod-product-compliance
Lightning Source LLC
Chambersburg PA
CBHW060306100426

42742CB00011B/1887